WORDS
YOUR OWN

An Early Christian
Guide to the Psalms

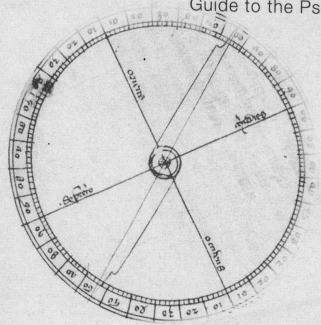

BENJAMIN
WAYMAN

PARACLETE PRESS
BREWSTER, MASSACHUSETTS

2014 First printing

Make the Words Your Own: An Early Christian Guide to the Psalms

Copyright © 2014 by Benjamin Wayman

ISBN 978-1-61261-418-2

Library of Congress Cataloging-in-Publication Data

Wayman, Benjamin D.
  Make the words your own : an early Christian guide to the Psalms / Benjamin D. Wayman ; foreword by Stanley Hauerwas ; afterword by Fr. David V. Meconi, SJ.
     pages cm
  Includes bibliographical references.
  ISBN 978-1-61261-418-2 (trade pbk.)
  1. Bible. Psalms—Devotional use. 2. Athanasius, Saint, Patriarch of Alexandria, -373. Opusculum in Psalmos. I. Title.
  BS1430.54.W39 2014
  223'.207—dc23   2014027599

10 9 8 7 6 5 4 3 2 1

Published by Paraclete Press
Brewster, Massachusetts
www.paracletepress.com

Printed in the United States of America

FOR CADEN, COLE, AND CONNOR

May you learn to make the words your own

CONTENTS

ONE
Psalms for the Suffering

TWO
Psalms for the Betrayed

THREE
Psalms for the Harassed

Foreword

We should not be surprised that Athanasius prayed the Psalms. Given his tumultuous life I am sure he needed every psalm we have in Scripture. Athanasius's observation that the Psalms embody the "whole experience of human life" is not only true but also a profound remark by someone whose life could only confirm that judgment. Athanasius, as Wayman helpfully reminds us, was a Christian who had a knack for making enemies. I suspect Athanasius was not surprised he had enemies. How could anyone who prays the Psalms as he did assume that one whose life is governed by God's law would not have enemies?

Accordingly Athanasius's guide to the Psalms is one of stark realism. His brief but pointed "aids" for the reading of the Psalms never invite the reader to engage in the illusion that if we just do what is right everything will work out the way we would like it to. Everything will work out, from Athanasius's perspective, but the "working out" will not necessarily be according to our desires, but rather to the glorification of God. But then that is what the Psalms are meant to do, that is, retrain our desires to see that we can want nothing more for ourselves than to have lives that glorify God.

That we have been created to glorify God is the presumption that makes intelligible Athanasius's recommendation that when we ask God for mercy we should praise him by singing Psalm 67. After all the Psalms for Athanasius is the songbook of the church. For Athanasius Christians sing their way into existence. Wayman is, therefore, quite right to emphasize the importance of words for Athanasius. By the singing of the words we become what we sing. We become what we sing because the Psalms do not so much give voice to what we are, but rather, they make us who we were created to be.

The words matter because they participate in the One that is the Word. For Athanasius not only does Jesus pray the Psalms, but also by praying the Psalms we discover Jesus. Athanasius's description of Psalm 22 dramatically makes this clear: "Psalm 22 describes the nature of the death from the lips of the Savior himself. . . . When he speaks of hands and feet being pierced, what else is meant than the cross? After presenting all these things the Psalter adds that the Lord suffers these things not for himself, but for our sake." Not only does Christ pray the Psalms, but Christ is the Father's Psalm offered so that by praying the Psalms we may be redeemed.

So to learn to pray the Psalms is a discipline that can free us from the narcissism that grips our lives, particularly in our day. We should be truly grateful to Benjamin Wayman for rescuing Athanasius's *Letter to Marcellinus*. In his lovely introduction to Athanasius's *The Incarnation of the Word of God*, C. S. Lewis observes that he often finds doctrinal books more helpful in devotion than devotional books. He does so, he explains, because he finds his heart sings when working his way through a tough bit of theology and that is not the case with books of devotion. I think Lewis might well find that Athanasius's *Letter to Marcellinus* would make his heart sing because, as Wayman argues, this book defies the distinction between doctrine and devotion.

I am fortunate to be in a school where, during the academic year, every day begins with Morning Prayer after the Book of Common Prayer. One of the reasons I have found Morning Prayer so important is because the Psalms are so central to the structure of our time together. I think there are few mornings I do not hear something in the Psalms that surprises me, challenges me, and/or frightens me. Reading Athanasius's *Letter* occasioned the same set of responses. That, I take it, is the way it should be.

STANLEY HAUERWAS
Gilbert T. Rowe Professor of Theological Ethics
Duke Divinity School

Introduction

The Psalter was the essential prayer book of the early church. Several factors contributed to the significance of Psalms in the prayer of the early church, not the least of which were the awareness that Christ himself prayed the Psalms and that its words became his own in his daily life. Nearly half of the Psalms quoted in the New Testament come from the very mouth of Christ. Psalms, in fact, is the most frequently cited Old Testament book in the New Testament and remained of central importance in early church practice. One scholar notes, "By Athanasius's time the memorization of the Psalms by many Christians and their habitual use as songs in worship by all Christians we know about were matters of longstanding tradition."[1] Psalms were used in the Eucharistic celebration, the preaching of the Word, the Daily Office, and even wedding and funeral services.[2] The everyday use of Psalms was prevalent in the early church.

A request for guidance from a sickly parishioner is what elicited a letter from Saint Athanasius, the great Alexandrian bishop whose direction for how to read the Psalms would be followed by Christians for years to come. It was fitting that Athanasius should write such a guide not only because Psalms was the book to which Marcellinus had committed special attention, nor even because of Athanasius's close acquaintance with the Psalter over a lifetime of meditating on its words, but also because Psalms was the prayer book of the church and Athanasius was a pastor.

Athanasius the Pastor-Theologian

This book brings you "face-to-face" with one of the greatest pastors of the early church, Athanasius of Alexandria (ca. 295–373). You will meet Athanasius in his own words and, hopefully, you will find him an accessible and wise guide for reading the Psalms. As C. S. Lewis once wrote, "firsthand knowledge is not only more worth acquiring than secondhand knowledge, but is usually much easier and more delightful to acquire."[3] Lewis was writing about Athanasius's classic work *On the Incarnation*, but the same is true for his letter to Marcellinus concerning the Psalms.

Athanasius's *Letter to Marcellinus, On the Interpretation of the Psalms* (ca. 367) is the earliest surviving Christian guide for personal devotion on the Psalms.[4] Despite having been written by perhaps the best-known figure of fourth-century Christianity (in his time, as well as our own), the work is rarely read or remembered today.[5] This was not always so.

Athanasius's letter was once cherished by the church and appears to be summarized in Saint Basil of Caesarea's (ca. 330–79) own prologue to Psalm 1. Basil's debt to Athanasius's letter can be seen not only in his précis of the main ideas from the letter,[6] but as well in his emphasis on the use of the Psalter for personal devotion. Basil states, "The book, in a word, is a treasury of sound teaching, and provides for every individual need. It heals the old hurts of souls, and brings about recovery where the wound is fresh. It wins the part that is sick and preserves that which is sound."[7] Basil's general thesis echoes that of Athanasius, who similarly emphasizes the instructional nature of the Psalms and their suitability for personal application when he states in his letter, "The psalms are composed in such a way that whoever is praying can find the movements and the condition of his own soul and, further, is provided with the model and the teaching for each of these states."[8] It appears that even Basil the Great had a copy of Athanasius's letter before him as he put to papyrus his own thoughts on the Psalms.

Not long after Athanasius died, Christians continued to hold his letter in high standing. It was given pride of place as an introduction to the Psalms in the *Alexandrinus*, a codex dated to the first half of the fifth century and one of the earliest and most complete manuscripts of the Bible. Scholars have established the authenticity of Athanasius's letter and believe that the text preserved in the *Alexandrinus* "preserves the original wording of Athanasius's treatise."[9] The letter is thus a rare artifact from early Christianity.

Christians in the Middle Ages and premodern times alike highly esteemed Athanasius's guidance to the Psalter. Patristic scholar Everett Ferguson notes that the letter

> was fairly widely circulated in the Middle Ages as an introduction to the Psalms. This is especially true of excerpts from the letter, known as *Opusculum in Psalmos.* . . . This section of the treatise applying the Psalms to personal circumstances of life may be the most original as well as most influential contribution made by the letter.[10]

The bulk of the material gleaned from Athanasius's letter and used to construct this *Guide to the Psalms* has been taken from the *Opusculum in Psalmos.*

But for both everyday Christians and patristic scholars today, the letter has been largely forgotten.[11] There are several causes for this, not the least of which is that Athanasius's powerful personality and prominence as *the* theologian of the fourth century has long eclipsed his more explicitly pastoral qualities and contributions. As one expert remarks, "Only a very determined man could have stood against emperors and councils of bishops, endured five exiles, and fought off numerous false accusations, all in defense of the gospel."[12] Within a generation or two after his death, legends of Athanasius's boyhood emulation of a bishop performing a baptism and, later, his refusal to marry as a young man despite his mother's repeated attempts to find him a bride were cemented in the minds of early Christians and have served "to identify Athanasius as a man marked out from his youth for greatness."[13] Athanasius's public activities have overshadowed his more pastoral work in the church's memory. But it is his pastoral concern that motivates his politics, disciplines his doctrinal writings, and animates his *Festal Letters*, *Life of Antony*, and *Letter to Marcellinus*.

Athanasius was born and raised in a pivotal time of the church's history, spanning from the persecution of Christians under the emperor Diocletian and the rise of Constantine to the first general council at Nicaea in 325 and the church's embroiled attempts to make sense of that council.[14] This time frame includes more specifically the first disagreement between Athanasius's mentor Alexander (bishop of Alexandria from 312–328) and the controversial Alexandrian priest Arius (ca. 250–336) sometime between 318 and 320, and what would become even more acutely Athanasius's own debate. This doctrinal battle concerned the divinity of the Son and how to reconcile such a claim with an insistence on monotheism, the clarification of which consumed the energies of a church that organized in several camps along complex ecclesial, social, and theological lines. As church histories took shape in the wake of the crisis, Athanasius emerged from the fourth century as "the Father of Orthodoxy," a title that was only enhanced by his opponents such as the pagan emperor Julian, who charged that he was a "disturber of the peace and enemy of the gods."[15] Athanasius's prominence as a leading theologian was inseparable from his visibility as a political figure, and so on five occasions he was expelled from his post as bishop of Alexandria and sent into exile.[16]

Even in exile, Athanasius actively participated in the church's doctrinal deliberations, strengthened its bond with the monastic world, and worked for peace across Christendom.[17] This can be observed, for example, in his *Discourses Against the Arians* (second exile, Rome),[18] *Life of Antony* (third exile, Egyptian desert),[19] and his letter to the Christians in Antioch (written in the short period between the third and fourth exiles).[20] Athanasius was an international figure known throughout the East and West, to emperors and desert monks alike. He served as the bishop of Alexandria for forty-six years, more than a third of which he spent in exile. Athanasius was thus no stranger to suffering, betrayal, and harassment.

And so it is understandable that a man so gifted with theological and political abilities would be a marked man, not only by those in power during his time, but also by later historians and theologians who sought and continue to seek to recover our larger-than-life bishop of Alexandria. These recoveries have mostly neglected Athanasius's role as pastor, and so it is his primary identity as a pastor that informs this book.[21]

Athanasius was one of the best-known pastors of his time and is today perhaps the most accessible early Christian guide for a prayerful reading of the Psalms. In his own time, he cared for "the most influential" congregation of the fourth century.[22] His church in Alexandria was one of the four major centers of early Christianity, and was a major contributor in the development of early Christian thought and life.

The modern division between pastors and theologians would have been unthinkable for a pastor-theologian such as Athanasius. Modern scholarship has been right to underline Athanasius's contributions as a theologian, but he was also a caring pastor, as is evidenced throughout his writings.[23] To be sure, Athanasius's pastoral concern in no way diminishes the theological rigor of his *Letter to Marcellinus, On the Interpretation of the Psalms.*[24]

In this pastoral letter, Athanasius commends the sickly Marcellinus for applying himself to the Psalms during his illness.[25] He assures Marcellinus that

> in the Psalter . . . you learn about *yourself*. You find depicted in it all the movements of your soul, all its changes, its ups and downs, its failures and recoveries. Moreover, whatever your particular need or trouble, from this same book you can select a form of words to fit it, so that you do not merely hear and then pass on, but learn the way to remedy your ill.[26]

In other words, for Athanasius, the very words of the Psalms have the power to heal and form one as a disciple.

Whether it is pastoral care for a parishioner that evokes his frequent commentary on human suffering or whether it is his own life experience, Athanasius repeatedly mentions the specific care in the Psalms for those who suffer. Athanasius writes, "In the Psalms it is written and inscribed how one must bear sufferings, what one must say to one suffering afflictions, and what to say after afflictions, how each person is tested, and what the words of those who hope in God are."[27] These are the words of one who has suffered much himself and has received through the Psalms both comfort and healing.

It is also pastorally significant that Athanasius affirms Marcellinus in his eagerness to understand the meanings of each psalm. Not only does he demonstrate care for Marcellinus in his illness, but he also commends his desire to understand the church's Scripture and be formed in Christian virtue. Athanasius accordingly underlines a special grace of the Psalms for those like Marcellinus who "pursue virtue" when he states, "All the divine scripture is a teacher of virtue and true faith, but the book of Psalms has also the image somehow of the very course of the life of souls. Just as he who approaches a king is prescribed a certain form and certain words, lest saying the wrong things he be ejected as rude, even so the divine book . . . teaches the readers by its words."[28] By placing a premium on the actual wording of the Psalms as a template for developing Christian virtue and faith, Athanasius composed a pastoral guide to the Psalms that remains to this day as valuable as it was in his own time.[29]

By the year 367 Athanasius was a mature pastor and well-formed interpreter of Scripture, and it was likely then that he composed his *Letter to Marcellinus*.[30] This manual for praying the Psalms was undoubtedly informed and shaped by his several years of exile in the desert with Egyptian monks whose every day was shaped by praying the Psalms.[31]

Scholars have underlined the importance of Athanasius's letter for understanding the early Christian interpretation of the Psalms.[32] Indeed, it is exegetically significant that Athanasius affirms rather than scolds Marcellinus for his request to understand *each* psalm. This interpretive approach is also valuable for practicing Christians today. Given that my primary purpose is to present Athanasius's guide as an aid for contemporary Christians, what I most want to highlight about Athanasius's teaching is his understanding of Psalms as a deeply personal vehicle for prayer and spiritual formation, unlike anything else in Scripture. He writes, "The Book of the Psalms possesses a certain grace all of its own and an exceptional quality of perceptiveness. For besides the characteristics it has in common with the other books [of Scripture], it possesses an extraordinary grace peculiar to itself—it reflects the movements of each soul, its changes and amendments, all represented and portrayed within the book itself."[33] In other words, Psalms is a kind of mirror of our selves, which provides us with the words both to understand and express our deepest emotions.

Athanasius's understanding of the Psalms is both common and unique among early Christian pastors. On the one hand, his view that the Psalms may be used as a personal prayer book was common in the early church. On the other hand, his teaching on the Psalms uniquely offers a personal and experiential guide for nearly every psalm.[34] By outlining the way in which the words "become like a mirror" to the one saying them, helping one "to understand in them the emotions of his own soul and thus perceiving them to explain them,"[35] Athanasius offers readers an approach to the Psalter that is self-reflective and, for those who are willing, transformative.

Athanasius's letter teaches Christians of his time as well as ours to make the words of the Psalms our own. Unlike any other book of Scripture, this is the special use of the Psalter. He explains that in the Psalms, "each person sings what has been written as about himself or herself, not at all as if receiving and reciting what was intended for someone else; they take it as their own, as if the words were theirs, and offer it to God as though they had composed the words themselves."[36] A *"self-involving discourse"* with God, Athanasius's program for reading the Psalms "draws us into the world of the text and demands response."[37] We are not to read from a distance, as mere spectators or disinterested third parties. His conviction rather is that "for every person whatsoever, we may find the divine songs appropriate for us and for the states of emotional turmoil or stability."[38] So, with Athanasius as a trusted pastor to lead us, the following guide presents twenty-first-century Christians with the opportunity to read the Psalms afresh with a mature disciple and saint.

Making the Words Your Own

Before offering instruction on how to use the following *Guide to the Psalms*, I want to say a word about Athanasius's theology of words and why we should make the words of the Psalms our own.[39] Athanasius's position that we make the words of the Psalms our own is a theological conviction, and one that is worth unpacking in some detail.

Earlier I noted the importance that Athanasius attributes to saying the actual words of the Psalms. This requires a bit of explanation, particularly given the fact that many Christians today regard extemporaneous prayer as the most authentic, and hence most powerful, form of prayer. Athanasius thinks otherwise, and this is largely due to two beliefs he holds about the Psalms. First, he believes that through the Psalms, one learns "the emotions and dispositions of souls, finding in the Psalms also the healing and correction of each emotion."[40] Second, one must say the *actual wording* of the Psalms if one is to be availed of their true power. The first belief, that the Psalms provide self-revealing and self-reforming discourse, has already been discussed, and so I wish to focus on the latter point in finer detail.

Already we had a glimpse of Athanasius's preference for the actual wording of the Psalms: it is like using the script one would be wise to use when coming before a king. A careless or misinterpreted word could have deadly consequences in such a situation. Athanasius later insists that "it is not for our actions only that we must give an account before the Judge, but also for our every idle word."[41] But despite its importance, there is more to Athanasius's theology of words than the appeasement of the Divine Judge. For Athanasius, one should recite the Psalms without embellishment or change. Stick to the words, he says, "so that the men who ministered these words might recognize them as their own and join with us in prayer. Or rather, let him use these words in order that the Spirit who spoke in the holy men, perceiving the words which he inspired to resound in them, might come to our assistance."[42] Thus Athanasius gives two more reasons for praying in the actual words of the Psalms: (1) these are the same words given to us by the saints, who will recognize them as their own and join us in our prayer; and (2) these are the words given to us by God, who is more likely to come to our aid because of their divine origin.

Athanasius expands on both reasons. In support of the first he explains, "For as the saints' lives are lovelier than any others, so too their words are better than ever ours can be, and of much more avail, provided only they be uttered from a righteous heart."[43] For contemporary Christians who object to such a seemingly elitist view of prayer, Athanasius's following reasoning invites reconsideration.[44] He draws first on the letter to the Hebrews to make his case and accordingly argues that in saying these words the saints "overcame kingdoms, enforced justice, obtained promises, stopped the mouths of lions, quenched mighty fires, escaped the edge of the sword, from weakness came to strength, became mighty in battle, routed foreign enemies, and women received back their dead through resurrection" (Heb. 11:33–35).[45] Athanasius then gives several more examples of other saints, living in Old Testament times and perhaps even his own, who by saying the words of the Psalms were quickly aided by God.[46]

Athanasius's second reason concerns God's relation and proximity to the words of the Psalms. For Athanasius, God's attention and willingness to answer those who pray in the words of the Psalms is due to the divine status of the words themselves, which is the explanation Athanasius gives for their power to put demons to flight. Athanasius states, "For *the Lord himself is in the words of Scripture*, and it is him whom they cannot endure: 'I beg you, do not torment me before the time' (Luke 8:28). And thus they were being destroyed seeing the Lord present."[47] For Athanasius, God is in the very words of the Psalter. Given these beliefs about the words of the Psalms, Athanasius's insistence that no one supplement or substitute its words should be seen as theologically informed.

To be clear, even though Athanasius considers the words of the Psalms to be personally applicable, spoken by the saints, and divine, these words must flow from lives of obedience to Christ in order for them to be efficacious. Near the close of his letter to Marcellinus, Athanasius is careful to underscore that the words of the Psalms must be accompanied by a holy life, empowered by the Holy Spirit. He explains, for example, that sin defuses the power of the Psalter's words because "there is need of faith and sincere motives in order for the law to cooperate in the things prayed for."[48] Put differently, the words of the Psalms must be *lived*. And when one lives a holy life, the power of the words of the Psalter cannot be overcome, for the demons "fear the words of the saints, and they cannot endure them."[49]

In like manner, Athanasius concludes his letter to Marcellinus by advising him, "And you, meditating on these words and reading the Psalms thus with understanding, 'being led by the Spirit,' will be able to understand the meaning in each. Emulate such a life as the holy men inspired of God had who spoke these words."[50] Equipped with an understanding of each psalm and the manner by which to appropriate such revelation personally, Marcellinus (and we) are invited to make the words of the Psalms our own as we become like the saints who have gone before us.[51]

How to use Athanasius's *Guide*

The following *Guide to the Psalms* is structured for both private and communal use.[52] As I mentioned earlier, it stands in a long history of Christians who have appropriated Athanasius's counsel to Marcellinus on the Psalms. The first four chapters comprise psalms for the suffering, the betrayed, the harassed, and the guilty, and particularly apply to those in times of acute need. The last four chapters include psalms for the thankful, for reflection, for instruction, and for daily living, and so may be considered appropriate for study or worship. The final chapter, for example, "Psalms for Daily Living," may be understood as one especially suited for the Daily Office.[53] Thus, Athanasius's *Guide* may be used as a daily prayer book, a manual for studying the Psalms, or a gracious gift in a time of need.

By referring to this book as "Athanasius's *Guide*," I follow Athanasius himself, who in his letter refers to the Psalms as "this guide" for holy living.[54] Athanasius prescribes a personalized and devotional reading of the Psalms as a guide for Christian discipleship. His instruction is worth quoting at length.

> It is necessary, my child, that everyone coming to this book read it with sincerity since the whole of it is inspired by God; and then select from it, as from the fruits of a blessed garden, what is useful as the need is perceived. For it is my opinion that the whole experience of human life, the disposition of the soul, and the movements of the reasoning faculties are encompassed in the words of this book, and that nothing outside of this is found in human life . . . in all these circumstances he has instructions in the divine psalms; let him choose from among all these expressions, which have been written as his own and, according to that wording, offer them to the Lord.[55]

Athanasius provides the reader a seasoned interpretation of each psalm in just a few sentences, which can be applied to the reader's personal life situation. In fact, he explicitly encourages such personal application. So, in what follows, the chapter themes are my own, but are based on the content of Athanasius's counsel for each psalm or group of psalms. My intention is that of Athanasius: that the reader will find here a rich model for a self-transforming reading of the Psalms. Athanasius says it best:

> The whole of every Psalm is spoken and composed by the Spirit, so . . . the movements of our souls may be understood. All of them are said about us, and *the words are to be assumed as our very own*, as a reminder of the movements of the soul, and as an amendment of our daily conduct, and so what has been expressed in the psalms can be for us as models and patterns.[56]

Athanasius instructs us to personally apply the Psalms, the practice of which conforms our lives to Christ.[57] Through praying the words of the Psalter *"as our very own,"* we learn a new language that makes possible a new life in Christ.[58] Thus, we become what we pray.

Critical Note

St. Athanasius's *Guide to the Psalms* is culled from the material largely found in chapters 14 through 26 of the *Epistola ad Marcellinum*. The Greek text is that of Migne's Patrologia Graeca (PG), volume 27, columns 12–45. Athanasius posits multiple applications for some psalms, and so in such cases I have selected the use that lends itself to the greatest specificity. So, for example, where Athanasius provides three uses for Psalm 24, the *Guide* features the one with the guidance most solely focused on Psalm 24 (giving thanks on Sunday), rather than its use in concert with Psalm 19 (regarding God's providence), or its coupling with Psalm 47 (referring to Christ's ascension). The reader will see, however, that the *Guide* leaves intact Athanasius's full counsel pertaining to each situation. Thus where Psalm 19 is presented, Athanasius's mention of Psalm 24 remains included.

In my translation of Athanasius's guidance in the letter I have aimed to keep two goals in focus: first, fidelity to Athanasius's syntax without sacrificing his meaning, and second, to render Athanasius's direction accessible for Christians today. The danger is that by presenting Athanasius's counsel more colloquially we should forget that he is centuries removed from us linguistically and culturally. The danger is worth the risk, I think, because the reward of following Athanasius in a personal and self-transforming reading of the Psalms far outweighs whatever may have been lost in translation.

Athanasius used the Greek translation of the Old Testament known as the Septuagint (LXX), in which the numbering of the Psalms does not always agree with the numbering found in the Hebrew and in our modern translations. The numbers agree only in Psalms 1–8 and Psalms 148–150. This is because Psalm 9 in the LXX combines our Psalms 9 and 10 and the LXX's Psalm 113 combines our Psalms 114 and 115; while the LXX's Psalms 114 and 115 divide our Psalm 116, and the LXX's Psalms 146 and 147 divide our Psalm 147. These two combinations and two divisions explain why both the Hebrew text (and ours) and the LXX have a total of 150 Psalms, despite the LXX's addition of Psalm 151. I should state as well that the LXX text sometimes differs from ours, and yet even a comparison of modern English translations reveals the fact that the Hebrew text poses a great many problems of translation. Finally, the reader may also note that the verse numbers in the Book of Common Prayer (BCP), which is the version of the Psalter used in the following *Guide*, and those in the New Revised Standard Version (NRSV) do not always correspond. For example, for the conversion of Psalm 116 the BCP divides the Psalm into verses 1–8 and verses 9–17, whereas in the NRSV the division is between verses 1–9 and 10–19. Similarly, for Psalm 147 the division in the BCP is between verses 1–12 and 13–21, whereas the NRSV divides the Psalm into verses 1–11 and 12–20. None of this need concern the reader, and where the problems become important, they will be indicated in the *Guide*. Rather, the reader should simply note that I have converted the numbering of Athanasius's LXX version of the Psalms to that of the BCP to allow for ease of reading.

ONE

Psalms for the Suffering

∽ PSALM 12

When you see the arrogance of the crowd and evil increasing such that nothing is considered holy by the people, run to the Lord and say Psalm 12.

Help me, LORD, for there is no godly one left;
  the faithful have vanished from among us.

Everyone speaks falsely with his neighbor;
  with a smooth tongue they speak from a double heart.

Oh, that the LORD would cut off all smooth tongues,
  and close the lips that utter proud boasts!

Those who say, "With our tongue will we prevail;
  our lips are our own; who is lord over us?"

"Because the needy are oppressed,
and the poor cry out in misery,
  I will rise up," says the LORD,
  "and give them the help they long for."

The words of the LORD are pure words,
  like silver refined from ore
  and purified seven times in the fire.

O LORD, watch over us
  and save us from this generation for ever.

The wicked prowl on every side,
  and that which is worthless is highly prized by everyone.

ᔔ PSALM 20

When you see others suffering, comfort them by praying for them with
the words in Psalm 20.

May the LORD answer you in the day of trouble,
the Name of the God of Jacob defend you;

Send you help from his holy place
and strengthen you out of Zion;

Remember all your offerings
and accept your burnt sacrifice;

Grant you your heart's desire
and prosper all your plans.

We will shout for joy at your victory
and triumph in the Name of our God;
may the LORD grant all your requests.

Now I know that the LORD gives victory to his anointed;
he will answer him out of his holy heaven,
with the victorious strength of his right hand.

Some put their trust in chariots and some in horses,
but we will call upon the Name of the LORD our God.

They collapse and fall down,
but we will arise and stand upright.

O LORD, give victory to the king
and answer us when we call.

∽ PSALM 22

Psalm 22 describes the nature of the death from the lips of the Savior himself. . . . When he speaks of hands and feet being pierced, what else is meant than the cross? After presenting all these things, the Psalter adds that the Lord suffers these things not for himself, but for our sake.

My God, my God, why have you forsaken me?
    and are so far from my cry
    and from the words of my distress?

O my God, I cry in the daytime, but you do not answer;
    by night as well, but I find no rest.

Yet you are the Holy One,
    enthroned upon the praises of Israel.

Our forefathers put their trust in you;
    they trusted, and you delivered them.

They cried out to you and were delivered;
    they trusted in you and were not put to shame.

But as for me, I am a worm and no man,
    scorned by all and despised by the people.

All who see me laugh me to scorn;
    they curl their lips and wag their heads, saying,

"He trusted in the Lord; let him deliver him;
    let him rescue him, if he delights in him."

Yet you are he who took me out of the womb,
    and kept me safe upon my mother's breast.

I have been entrusted to you ever since I was born;
    you were my God when I was still in my
        mother's womb.

Be not far from me, for trouble is near,
    and there is none to help.

Many young bulls encircle me;
    strong bulls of Bashan surround me.

They open wide their jaws at me,
    like a ravening and a roaring lion.

I am poured out like water;
all my bones are out of joint;
    my heart within my breast is melting wax.

My mouth is dried out like a pot-sherd;
my tongue sticks to the roof of my mouth;
    and you have laid me in the dust of the grave.

Packs of dogs close me in,
and gangs of evildoers circle around me;
    they pierce my hands and my feet;
    I can count all my bones.

They stare and gloat over me;
    they divide my garments among them;
    they cast lots for my clothing.

Be not far away, O Lord;
    you are my strength; hasten to help me.

Save me from the sword,
    my life from the power of the dog.

Save me from the lion's mouth,
    my wretched body from the horns of wild bulls.

I will declare your Name to my brethren;
    in the midst of the congregation I will praise you.

Praise the Lord, you that fear him;
    stand in awe of him, O offspring of Israel;
    all you of Jacob's line, give glory.

For he does not despise nor abhor the poor in their poverty;
neither does he hide his face from them;
>but when they cry to him he hears them.

My praise is of him in the great assembly;
>I will perform my vows in the presence of those who
>>worship him.

The poor shall eat and be satisfied,
and those who seek the Lord shall praise him:
>"May your heart live for ever!"

All the ends of the earth shall remember and turn to the LORD,
>and all the families of the nations shall bow before him.

For kingship belongs to the LORD;
>he rules over the nations.

To him alone all who sleep in the earth bow down in worship;
>all who go down to the dust fall before him.

My soul shall live for him;
my descendants shall serve him;
>they shall be known as the LORD's for ever.

They shall come and make known to a people yet unborn
>the saving deeds that he has done.

∽ PSALM 28

Since human nature is weak, if again the schemers are acting viciously
such that you have no rest from them, cry out to God saying the words
in Psalm 28.

O LORD, I call to you;
my Rock, do not be deaf to my cry;
>lest, if you do not hear me,
>>I become like those who go down to the Pit.

Hear the voice of my prayer when I cry out to you,
  when I lift up my hands to your holy of holies.

Do not snatch me away with the wicked or with the
            evildoers,
  who speak peaceably with their neighbors,
  while strife is in their hearts.

Repay them according to their deeds,
  and according to the wickedness of their actions.

According to the work of their hands repay them,
  and give them their just deserts.

They have no understanding of the LORD's doings,
nor of the works of his hands;
  therefore he will break them down and not
          build them up.

Blessed is the LORD!
  for he has heard the voice of my prayer.

The LORD is my strength and my shield;
  my heart trusts in him, and I have been helped;

Therefore my heart dances for joy,
  and in my song will I praise him.

The LORD is the strength of his people,
  a safe refuge for his anointed.

Save your people and bless your inheritance;
  shepherd them and carry them for ever.

○⁹ PSALM 40

If while your enemies are attacking you, you patiently endure the suffering
and want to learn the benefit of such endurance, sing Psalm 40.

I waited patiently upon the LORD;
   he stooped to me and heard my cry.

He lifted me out of the desolate pit, out of the mire and clay;
   he set my feet upon a high cliff and made my footing sure.

He put a new song in my mouth,
a song of praise to our God;
      many shall see, and stand in awe,
      and put their trust in the LORD.

Happy are they who trust in the LORD!
   they do not resort to evil spirits or turn to false gods.

Great things are they that you have done, O LORD my God!
how great your wonders and your plans for us!
   there is none who can be compared with you.

Oh, that I could make them known and tell them!
   but they are more than I can count.

In sacrifice and offering you take no pleasure
   (you have given me ears to hear you);

Burnt-offering and sin-offering you have not required,
   and so I said, "Behold, I come.

In the roll of the book it is written concerning me:
   'I love to do your will, O my God;
   your law is deep in my heart.'"

I proclaimed righteousness in the great congregation;
   behold, I did not restrain my lips;
   and that, O LORD, you know.

Your righteousness have I not hidden in my heart;
I have spoken of your faithfulness and your deliverance;
    I have not concealed your love and faithfulness from the
        great congregation.

You are the Lord;
do not withhold your compassion from me;
    let your love and your faithfulness keep me safe for ever.

For innumerable troubles have crowded upon me;
my sins have overtaken me, and I cannot see;
    they are more in number than the hairs of my head,
    and my heart fails me.

Be pleased, O Lord, to deliver me;
    O Lord, make haste to help me.

Let them be ashamed and altogether dismayed
who seek after my life to destroy it;
    let them draw back and be disgraced
    who take pleasure in my misfortune.

Let those who say "Aha!" and gloat over me be confounded,
    because they are ashamed.

Let all who seek you rejoice in you and be glad;
    let those who love your salvation continually say,
    "Great is the Lord!"

Though I am poor and afflicted,
    the Lord will have regard for me.

You are my helper and my deliverer;
    do not tarry, O my God.

෴ PSALM 42

If you have a deep longing for God and you hear your enemies mocking you, do not be troubled. Understand that such longing brings eternal blessing and comfort your soul with hope in God. In this way, relieving and lightening your suffering in life, say Psalm 42.

As the deer longs for the water-brooks,
    so longs my soul for you, O God.

My soul is athirst for God, athirst for the living God;
    when shall I come to appear before the presence of God?

My tears have been my food day and night,
    while all day long they say to me,
    "Where now is your God?"

I pour out my soul when I think on these things:
    how I went with the multitude and led them into the
        house of God,

With the voice of praise and thanksgiving,
    among those who keep holy-day.

Why are you so full of heaviness, O my soul?
    and why are you so disquieted within me?

Put your trust in God;
    for I will yet give thanks to him,
    who is the help of my countenance, and my God.

My soul is heavy within me;
    therefore I will remember you from the land of Jordan,
    and from the peak of Mizar among the heights of Hermon.

One deep calls to another in the noise of your cataracts;
    all your rapids and floods have gone over me.

The LORD grants his loving-kindness in the daytime;
    in the night season his song is with me,
    a prayer to the God of my life.

I will say to the God of my strength,
" Why have you forgotten me?
   and why do I go so heavily while the enemy
      oppresses me?"

While my bones are being broken,
   my enemies mock me to my face;

All day long they mock me
   and say to me, "Where now is your God?"

Why are you so full of heaviness, O my soul?
   and why are you so disquieted within me?

Put your trust in God;
   for I will yet give thanks to him,
   who is the help of my countenance, and my God.

∽ PSALM 69

Psalms 22 and 69 announce beforehand the divine cross and what great treachery the Savior experienced for our sake and how much he suffered.

Save me, O God,
   for the waters have risen up to my neck.

I am sinking in deep mire,
   and there is no firm ground for my feet.

I have come into deep waters,
   and the torrent washes over me.

I have grown weary with my crying;
my throat is inflamed;
   my eyes have failed from looking for my God.

Those who hate me without a cause are more than the hairs
　　　　of my head;
　　my lying foes who would destroy me are mighty.
　　Must I then give back what I never stole?

O God, you know my foolishness,
　　and my faults are not hidden from you.

Let not those who hope in you be put to shame through me,
　　　　Lord GOD of hosts;
　　let not those who seek you be disgraced because of me,
　　　　O God of Israel.

Surely, for your sake have I suffered reproach,
　　and shame has covered my face.

I have become a stranger to my own kindred,
　　an alien to my mother's children.

Zeal for your house has eaten me up;
　　the scorn of those who scorn you has fallen upon me.

I humbled myself with fasting,
　　but that was turned to my reproach.

I put on sack-cloth also,
　　and became a byword among them.

Those who sit at the gate murmur against me,
　　and the drunkards make songs about me.

But as for me, this is my prayer to you,
　　at the time you have set, O LORD:

"In your great mercy, O God,
　　answer me with your unfailing help.

Save me from the mire; do not let me sink;
　　let me be rescued from those who hate me
　　and out of the deep waters.

Let not the torrent of waters wash over me,
neither let the deep swallow me up;
    do not let the Pit shut its mouth upon me.

Answer me, O LORD, for your love is kind;
    in your great compassion, turn to me."

"Hide not your face from your servant;
    be swift and answer me, for I am in distress.

Draw near to me and redeem me;
    because of my enemies deliver me.

You know my reproach, my shame, and my dishonor;
    my adversaries are all in your sight."

Reproach has broken my heart, and it cannot be healed;
    I looked for sympathy, but there was none,
    for comforters, but I could find no one.

They gave me gall to eat,
    and when I was thirsty, they gave me vinegar to drink.

Let the table before them be a trap
    and their sacred feasts a snare.

Let their eyes be darkened, that they may not see,
    and give them continual trembling in their loins.

Pour out your indignation upon them,
    and let the fierceness of your anger overtake them.

Let their camp be desolate,
    and let there be none to dwell in their tents.

For they persecute him whom you have stricken
    and add to the pain of those whom you have pierced.

Lay to their charge guilt upon guilt,
    and let them not receive your vindication.

Let them be wiped out of the book of the living
>and not be written among the righteous.

As for me, I am afflicted and in pain;
>your help, O God, will lift me up on high.

I will praise the Name of God in song;
>I will proclaim his greatness with thanksgiving.

This will please the LORD more than an offering of oxen,
>more than bullocks with horns and hoofs.

The afflicted shall see and be glad;
>you who seek God, your heart shall live.

For the LORD listens to the needy,
>and his prisoners he does not despise.

Let the heavens and the earth praise him,
>the seas and all that moves in them;

For God will save Zion and rebuild the cities of Judah;
>they shall live there and have it in possession.

The children of his servants will inherit it,
>and those who love his Name will dwell therein.

ᵔ PSALM 73

When you see people who disregard God thriving in peace and living in prosperity and faithful people suffering affliction, say the words in Psalm 73 so that you will not be tripped and shaken from your course.

Truly, God is good to Israel,
>to those who are pure in heart.

But as for me, my feet had nearly slipped;
>I had almost tripped and fallen;

Because I envied the proud
    and saw the prosperity of the wicked:

For they suffer no pain,
    and their bodies are sleek and sound;

In the misfortunes of others they have no share;
    they are not afflicted as others are;

Therefore they wear their pride like a necklace
    and wrap their violence about them like a cloak.

Their iniquity comes from gross minds,
    and their hearts overflow with wicked thoughts.

They scoff and speak maliciously;
    out of their haughtiness they plan oppression.

They set their mouths against the heavens,
    and their evil speech runs through the world.

And so the people turn to them
    and find in them no fault.

They say, "How should God know?
    is there knowledge in the Most High?"

So then, these are the wicked;
    always at ease, they increase their wealth.

In vain have I kept my heart clean,
    and washed my hands in innocence.

I have been afflicted all day long,
    and punished every morning.

Had I gone on speaking this way,
    I should have betrayed the generation of your children.

When I tried to understand these things,
    it was too hard for me;

Until I entered the sanctuary of God
   and discerned the end of the wicked.

Surely, you set them in slippery places;
   you cast them down in ruin.

Oh, how suddenly do they come to destruction,
   come to an end, and perish from terror!

Like a dream when one awakens, O Lord,
   when you arise you will make their image vanish.

When my mind became embittered,
   I was sorely wounded in my heart.

I was stupid and had no understanding;
   I was like a brute beast in your presence.

Yet I am always with you;
   you hold me by my right hand.

You will guide me by your counsel,
   and afterwards receive me with glory.

Whom have I in heaven but you?
   and having you I desire nothing upon earth.

Though my flesh and my heart should waste away,
   God is the strength of my heart and my portion for ever.

Truly, those who forsake you will perish;
   you destroy all who are unfaithful.

But it is good for me to be near God;
   I have made the Lord GOD my refuge.

I will speak of all your works
   in the gates of the city of Zion.

⌒ PSALM 79

If enemies persist and rushing in, they profane the house of God, kill the saints, and throw their bodies to the birds of the air, suffer with those who are suffering and plead with God, so that you are not drawn into or overcome by their cruelty, by saying Psalm 79.

O God, the heathen have come into your inheritance;
they have profaned your holy temple;
　　they have made Jerusalem a heap of rubble.

They have given the bodies of your servants as food for the
　　　　　birds of the air,
　　and the flesh of your faithful ones to the beasts
　　　　of the field.

They have shed their blood like water on every side
　　　　of Jerusalem,
　　and there was no one to bury them.

We have become a reproach to our neighbors,
　　an object of scorn and derision to those around us.

How long will you be angry, O Lord?
　　will your fury blaze like fire for ever?

Pour out your wrath upon the heathen who have not
　　　　known you
　　and upon the kingdoms that have not called upon
　　　　your Name.

For they have devoured Jacob
　　and made his dwelling a ruin.

Remember not our past sins;
let your compassion be swift to meet us;
　　for we have been brought very low.

Help us, O God our Savior, for the glory of your Name;
　　deliver us and forgive us our sins, for your Name's sake.

Why should the heathen say, "Where is their God?"
    Let it be known among the heathen and in our sight
    that you avenge the shedding of your servants' blood.

Let the sorrowful sighing of the prisoners come before you,
    and by your great might spare those who are
        condemned to die.

May the revilings with which they reviled you, O Lord,
    return seven-fold into their bosoms.

For we are your people and the sheep of your pasture;
    we will give you thanks for ever
    and show forth your praise from age to age.

⤳ PSALM 91

When you want to encourage yourself and others in Christian living, since hope in God brings no regret but makes the soul fearless, praise God by saying the words in Psalm 91.

He who dwells in the shelter of the Most High,
    abides under the shadow of the Almighty.

He shall say to the LORD,
"You are my refuge and my stronghold,
    my God in whom I put my trust."

He shall deliver you from the snare of the hunter
    and from the deadly pestilence.

He shall cover you with his pinions,
and you shall find refuge under his wings;
    his faithfulness shall be a shield and buckler.

You shall not be afraid of any terror by night,
    nor of the arrow that flies by day;

Of the plague that stalks in the darkness,
    nor of the sickness that lays waste at mid-day.

A thousand shall fall at your side
and ten thousand at your right hand,
    but it shall not come near you.

Your eyes have only to behold
    to see the reward of the wicked.

Because you have made the LORD your refuge,
    and the Most High your habitation,

There shall no evil happen to you,
    neither shall any plague come near your dwelling.

For he shall give his angels charge over you,
    to keep you in all your ways.

They shall bear you in their hands,
    lest you dash your foot against a stone.

You shall tread upon the lion and adder;
    you shall trample the young lion and the serpent
        under your feet.

Because he is bound to me in love,
therefore will I deliver him;
    I will protect him, because he knows my Name.

He shall call upon me, and I will answer him;
    I am with him in trouble;
    I will rescue him and bring him to honor.

With long life will I satisfy him,
    and show him my salvation.

⌒ PSALM 102

Since our nature is weak, if due to the hardships of life you become
like a beggar who has lost hope and you want to be comforted, you
have Psalm 102.

LORD, hear my prayer, and let my cry come before you;
　　hide not your face from me in the day of my trouble.

Incline your ear to me;
　　when I call, make haste to answer me,

For my days drift away like smoke,
　　and my bones are hot as burning coals.

My heart is smitten like grass and withered,
　　so that I forget to eat my bread.

Because of the voice of my groaning
　　I am but skin and bones.

I have become like a vulture in the wilderness,
　　like an owl among the ruins.

I lie awake and groan;
　　I am like a sparrow, lonely on a house-top.

My enemies revile me all day long,
　　and those who scoff at me have taken an oath against me.

For I have eaten ashes for bread
　　and mingled my drink with weeping.
Because of your indignation and wrath
　　you have lifted me up and thrown me away.

My days pass away like a shadow,
　　and I wither like the grass.

But you, O LORD, endure for ever,
　　and your Name from age to age.

You will arise and have compassion on Zion,
for it is time to have mercy upon her;
   indeed, the appointed time has come.

For your servants love her very rubble,
   and are moved to pity even for her dust.

The nations shall fear your Name, O LORD,
   and all the kings of the earth your glory.

For the LORD will build up Zion,
   and his glory will appear.

He will look with favor on the prayer of the homeless;
   he will not despise their plea.

Let this be written for a future generation,
   so that a people yet unborn may praise the LORD.

For the LORD looked down from his holy place on high;
   from the heavens he beheld the earth;

That he might hear the groan of the captive
   and set free those condemned to die;

That they may declare in Zion the Name of the LORD,
   and his praise in Jerusalem;

When the peoples are gathered together,
   and the kingdoms also, to serve the LORD.

He has brought down my strength before my time;
   he has shortened the number of my days;

And I said, "O my God,
do not take me away in the midst of my days;
   your years endure throughout all generations.

In the beginning, O LORD, you laid the foundations
      of the earth,
   and the heavens are the work of your hands;

They shall perish, but you will endure;
they all shall wear out like a garment;
  as clothing you will change them,
  and they shall be changed;

But you are always the same,
  and your years will never end.

The children of your servants shall continue,
  and their offspring shall stand fast in your sight."

∽ PSALM 119

If anyone is concerned for those who suffer let him speak these words.
In this way, he will show his true and firm faith and help them because
when God sees this, he offers the perfect remedy to those in need.
Knowing this, the holy one said in Psalm 119. . . .

Happy are they whose way is blameless,
  who walk in the law of the LORD!

Happy are they who observe his decrees
  and seek him with all their hearts!

Who never do any wrong,
  but always walk in his ways.

You laid down your commandments,
  that we should fully keep them.

Oh, that my ways were made so direct
  that I might keep your statutes!

Then I should not be put to shame,
  when I regard all your commandments.

I will thank you with an unfeigned heart,
  when I have learned your righteous judgments.

I will keep your statutes;
  do not utterly forsake me.

How shall a young man cleanse his way?
  By keeping to your words.

With my whole heart I seek you;
  let me not stray from your commandments.

I treasure your promise in my heart,
  that I may not sin against you.

Blessed are you, O LORD;
  instruct me in your statutes.

With my lips will I recite
  all the judgments of your mouth.

I have taken greater delight in the way of your decrees
  than in all manner of riches.

I will meditate on your commandments
  and give attention to your ways.

My delight is in your statutes;
  I will not forget your word.

Deal bountifully with your servant,
  that I may live and keep your word.
Open my eyes, that I may see
  the wonders of your law.

I am a stranger here on earth;
  do not hide your commandments from me.

My soul is consumed at all times
  with longing for your judgments.

You have rebuked the insolent;
  cursed are they who stray from your commandments!

Turn from me shame and rebuke,
    for I have kept your decrees.

Even though rulers sit and plot against me,
    I will meditate on your statutes.

For your decrees are my delight,
    and they are my counselors.

My soul cleaves to the dust;
    give me life according to your word.

I have confessed my ways, and you answered me;
    instruct me in your statutes.

Make me understand the way of your commandments,
    that I may meditate on your marvelous works.

My soul melts away for sorrow;
    strengthen me according to your word.

Take from me the way of lying;
    let me find grace through your law.

I have chosen the way of faithfulness;
    I have set your judgments before me.

I hold fast to your decrees;
    O LORD, let me not be put to shame.

I will run the way of your commandments,
    for you have set my heart at liberty.

Teach me, O LORD, the way of your statutes,
    and I shall keep it to the end.

Give me understanding, and I shall keep your law;
    I shall keep it with all my heart.

Make me go in the path of your commandments,
    for that is my desire.

Incline my heart to your decrees
  and not to unjust gain.

Turn my eyes from watching what is worthless;
  give me life in your ways.

Fulfill your promise to your servant,
  which you make to those who fear you.

Turn away the reproach which I dread,
  because your judgments are good.

Behold, I long for your commandments;
  in your righteousness preserve my life.

Let your loving-kindness come to me, O LORD,
  and your salvation, according to your promise.

Then shall I have a word for those who taunt me,
  because I trust in your words.

Do not take the word of truth out of my mouth,
  for my hope is in your judgments.

I shall continue to keep your law;
  I shall keep it for ever and ever.

I will walk at liberty,
  because I study your commandments.

I will tell of your decrees before kings
  and will not be ashamed.

I delight in your commandments,
  which I have always loved.

I will lift up my hands to your commandments,
  and I will meditate on your statutes.

Remember your word to your servant,
  because you have given me hope.

This is my comfort in my trouble,
　　that your promise gives me life.

The proud have derided me cruelly,
　　but I have not turned from your law.

When I remember your judgments of old,
　　O LORD, I take great comfort.

I am filled with a burning rage,
　　because of the wicked who forsake your law.

Your statutes have been like songs to me
　　wherever I have lived as a stranger.

I remember your Name in the night, O LORD,
　　and dwell upon your law.

This is how it has been with me,
　　because I have kept your commandments.

You only are my portion, O LORD;
　　I have promised to keep your words.

I entreat you with all my heart,
　　be merciful to me according to your promise.

I have considered my ways
　　and turned my feet toward your decrees.

I hasten and do not tarry
　　to keep your commandments.

Though the cords of the wicked entangle me,
　　I do not forget your law.

At midnight I will rise to give you thanks,
　　because of your righteous judgments.

I am a companion of all who fear you
　　and of those who keep your commandments.

The earth, O LORD, is full of your love;
    instruct me in your statutes.

O LORD, you have dealt graciously with your servant,
    according to your word.

Teach me discernment and knowledge,
    for I have believed in your commandments.

Before I was afflicted I went astray,
    but now I keep your word.

You are good and you bring forth good;
    instruct me in your statutes.

The proud have smeared me with lies,
    but I will keep your commandments with my whole heart.

Their heart is gross and fat,
    but my delight is in your law.

It is good for me that I have been afflicted,
    that I might learn your statutes.

The law of your mouth is dearer to me
    than thousands in gold and silver.

Your hands have made me and fashioned me;
    give me understanding, that I may learn your
        commandments.

Those who fear you will be glad when they see me,
    because I trust in your word.

I know, O LORD, that your judgments are right
    and that in faithfulness you have afflicted me.

Let your loving-kindness be my comfort,
    as you have promised to your servant.

Let your compassion come to me, that I may live,
    for your law is my delight.

Let the arrogant be put to shame, for they wrong me
                    with lies;
    but I will meditate on your commandments.

Let those who fear you turn to me,
    and also those who know your decrees.

Let my heart be sound in your statutes,
    that I may not be put to shame.

My soul has longed for your salvation;
    I have put my hope in your word.

My eyes have failed from watching for your promise,
    and I say, "When will you comfort me?"

I have become like a leather flask in the smoke,
    but I have not forgotten your statutes.

How much longer must I wait?
    when will you give judgment against those who
            persecute me?

The proud have dug pits for me;
    they do not keep your law.

All your commandments are true;
    help me, for they persecute me with lies.

They had almost made an end of me on earth,
    but I have not forsaken your commandments.

In your loving-kindness, revive me,
    that I may keep the decrees of your mouth.

O LORD, your word is everlasting;
    it stands firm in the heavens.

Your faithfulness remains from one generation to another;
　　you established the earth, and it abides.

By your decree these continue to this day,
　　for all things are your servants.

If my delight had not been in your law,
　　I should have perished in my affliction.

I will never forget your commandments,
　　because by them you give me life.

I am yours; oh, that you would save me!
　　for I study your commandments.

Though the wicked lie in wait for me to destroy me,
　　I will apply my mind to your decrees.

I see that all things come to an end,
　　but your commandment has no bounds.

Oh, how I love your law!
　　all the day long it is in my mind.

Your commandment has made me wiser than my enemies,
　　and it is always with me.

I have more understanding than all my teachers,
　　for your decrees are my study.

I am wiser than the elders,
　　because I observe your commandments.

I restrain my feet from every evil way,
　　that I may keep your word.

I do not shrink from your judgments,
　　because you yourself have taught me.

How sweet are your words to my taste!
　　they are sweeter than honey to my mouth.

Through your commandments I gain understanding;
    therefore I hate every lying way.

Your word is a lantern to my feet
    and a light upon my path.

I have sworn and am determined
    to keep your righteous judgments.

I am deeply troubled;
    preserve my life, O LORD, according to your word.

Accept, O LORD, the willing tribute of my lips,
    and teach me your judgments.

My life is always in my hand,
    yet I do not forget your law.

The wicked have set a trap for me,
    but I have not strayed from your commandments.

Your decrees are my inheritance for ever;
    truly, they are the joy of my heart.

I have applied my heart to fulfill your statutes
    for ever and to the end.

I hate those who have a divided heart,
    but your law do I love.

You are my refuge and shield;
    my hope is in your word.

Away from me, you wicked!
    I will keep the commandments of my God.

Sustain me according to your promise, that I may live,
    and let me not be disappointed in my hope.

Hold me up, and I shall be safe,
    and my delight shall be ever in your statutes.

You spurn all who stray from your statutes;
    their deceitfulness is in vain.

In your sight all the wicked of the earth are but dross;
    therefore I love your decrees.

My flesh trembles with dread of you;
    I am afraid of your judgments.

I have done what is just and right;
    do not deliver me to my oppressors.

Be surety for your servant's good;
    let not the proud oppress me.

My eyes have failed from watching for your salvation
    and for your righteous promise.

Deal with your servant according to your loving-kindness
    and teach me your statutes.

I am your servant; grant me understanding,
    that I may know your decrees.

It is time for you to act, O LORD,
    for they have broken your law.

Truly, I love your commandments
    more than gold and precious stones.

I hold all your commandments to be right for me;
    all paths of falsehood I abhor.

Your decrees are wonderful;
    therefore I obey them with all my heart.

When your word goes forth it gives light;
    it gives understanding to the simple.

I open my mouth and pant;
    I long for your commandments.

Turn to me in mercy,
    as you always do to those who love your Name.

Steady my footsteps in your word;
    let no iniquity have dominion over me.

Rescue me from those who oppress me,
    and I will keep your commandments.

Let your countenance shine upon your servant
    and teach me your statutes.

My eyes shed streams of tears,
    because people do not keep your law.

You are righteous, O LORD,
    and upright are your judgments.

You have issued your decrees
    with justice and in perfect faithfulness.

My indignation has consumed me,
    because my enemies forget your words.

Your word has been tested to the uttermost,
    and your servant holds it dear.

I am small and of little account,
    yet I do not forget your commandments.

Your justice is an everlasting justice
    and your law is the truth.

Trouble and distress have come upon me,
    yet your commandments are my delight.

The righteousness of your decrees is everlasting;
    grant me understanding, that I may live.

I call with my whole heart;
    answer me, O LORD, that I may keep your statutes.

I call to you;
oh, that you would save me!
    I will keep your decrees.

Early in the morning I cry out to you,
    for in your word is my trust.

My eyes are open in the night watches,
    that I may meditate upon your promise.

Hear my voice, O LORD, according to your loving-kindness;
    according to your judgments, give me life.

They draw near who in malice persecute me;
    they are very far from your law.

You, O LORD, are near at hand,
    and all your commandments are true.

Long have I known from your decrees
    that you have established them for ever.

Behold my affliction and deliver me,
    for I do not forget your law.

Plead my cause and redeem me;
    according to your promise, give me life.

Deliverance is far from the wicked,
    for they do not study your statutes.

Great is your compassion, O LORD;
    preserve my life, according to your judgments.

There are many who persecute and oppress me,
    yet I have not swerved from your decrees.

I look with loathing at the faithless,
    for they have not kept your word.

See how I love your commandments!
  O LORD, in your mercy, preserve me.

The heart of your word is truth;
  all your righteous judgments endure for evermore.

Rulers have persecuted me without a cause,
  but my heart stands in awe of your word.

I am as glad because of your promise
  as one who finds great spoils.

As for lies, I hate and abhor them,
  but your law is my love.

Seven times a day do I praise you,
  because of your righteous judgments.

Great peace have they who love your law;
  for them there is no stumbling block.

I have hoped for your salvation, O LORD,
  and have fulfilled your commandments.

I have kept your decrees
  and I have loved them deeply.

I have kept your commandments and decrees,
  for all my ways are before you.

Let my cry come before you, O LORD;
  give me understanding, according to your word.

Let my supplication come before you;
  deliver me, according to your promise.

My lips shall pour forth your praise,
  when you teach me your statutes.

My tongue shall sing of your promise,
  for all your commandments are righteous.

Let your hand be ready to help me,
    for I have chosen your commandments.

I long for your salvation, O LORD,
    and your law is my delight.

Let me live, and I will praise you,
    and let your judgments help me.

I have gone astray like a sheep that is lost;
    search for your servant,
        for I do not forget your commandments.

TWO

Psalms for the Betrayed

∽ PSALM 3

When you are rejected by your own people, and you have many who rise up against you, say Psalm 3.

LORD, how many adversaries I have!
  how many there are who rise up against me!

How many there are who say of me,
  "There is no help for him in his God."

But you, O LORD, are a shield about me;
  you are my glory, the one who lifts up my head.

I call aloud upon the LORD,
  and he answers me from his holy hill;

I lie down and go to sleep;
  I wake again, because the LORD sustains me.

I do not fear the multitudes of people
  who set themselves against me all around.

Rise up, O LORD; set me free, O my God;
  surely, you will strike all my enemies across the face,
  you will break the teeth of the wicked.

Deliverance belongs to the LORD.
  Your blessing be upon your people!

∽ PSALM 7

If certain people plot against you, as Ahithophel did against David, and someone reports this to you, sing Psalm 7 and take courage in God, who will defend you.

O LORD my God, I take refuge in you;
    save and deliver me from all who pursue me;

Lest like a lion they tear me in pieces
    and snatch me away with none to deliver me.

O LORD my God, if I have done these things:
    if there is any wickedness in my hands,

If I have repaid my friend with evil,
    or plundered him who without cause is my enemy;

Then let my enemy pursue and overtake me,
    trample my life into the ground,
    and lay my honor in the dust.

Stand up, O LORD, in your wrath;
    rise up against the fury of my enemies.

Awake, O my God, decree justice;
    let the assembly of the peoples gather round you.

Be seated on your lofty throne, O Most High;
    O LORD, judge the nations.

Give judgment for me according to my
        righteousness, O LORD,
    and according to my innocence, O Most High.

Let the malice of the wicked come to an end,
but establish the righteous;
    for you test the mind and heart, O righteous God.

God is my shield and defense;
    he is the savior of the true in heart.

God is a righteous judge;
    God sits in judgment every day.

If they will not repent, God will whet his sword;
    he will bend his bow and make it ready.

He has prepared his weapons of death;
    he makes his arrows shafts of fire.

Look at those who are in labor with wickedness,
    who conceive evil, and give birth to a lie.

They dig a pit and make it deep
    and fall into the hole that they have made.

Their malice turns back upon their own head;
    their violence falls on their own scalp.

I will bear witness that the LORD is righteous;
    I will praise the Name of the LORD Most High.

⟋ PSALM 27

If your enemies violently attack you and become a crowd like soldiers encamped against you, looking down on you as though you were not anointed—and for this very reason they want to fight—do not cower in fear, but sing Psalm 27.

The LORD is my light and my salvation;
whom then shall I fear?
    the LORD is the strength of my life;
    of whom then shall I be afraid?

When evildoers came upon me to eat up my flesh,
    it was they, my foes and my adversaries,
        who stumbled and fell.

Though an army should encamp against me,
    yet my heart shall not be afraid;

And though war should rise up against me,
    yet will I put my trust in him.

One thing have I asked of the LORD;
one thing I seek;
    that I may dwell in the house of the LORD all the days
        of my life;

To behold the fair beauty of the LORD
    and to seek him in his temple.

For in the day of trouble he shall keep me safe
        in his shelter;
    he shall hide me in the secrecy of his dwelling
    and set me high upon a rock.

Even now he lifts up my head
    above my enemies round about me.

Therefore I will offer in his dwelling an oblation
with sounds of great gladness;
    I will sing and make music to the LORD.

Hearken to my voice, O LORD, when I call;
    have mercy on me and answer me.

You speak in my heart and say, "Seek my face."
    Your face, LORD, will I seek.

Hide not your face from me,
    nor turn away your servant in displeasure.

You have been my helper;
cast me not away;
    do not forsake me, O God of my salvation.

Though my father and my mother forsake me,
    the LORD will sustain me.

Show me your way, O LORD;
  lead me on a level path, because of my enemies.

Deliver me not into the hand of my adversaries,
  for false witnesses have risen up against me,
    and also those who speak malice.

What if I had not believed
that I should see the goodness of the LORD
    in the land of the living!

O tarry and await the LORD's pleasure;
be strong, and he shall comfort your heart;
  wait patiently for the Lord.

⌒ PSALM 31

When you see yourself being hated and rejected because of the truth
by all your friends and family, do not become discouraged when think-
ing either of them or yourself. And when you see your acquaintances
avoiding you, do not be alarmed, but withdraw from them, and looking
to your future in God, sing Psalm 31.

In you, O LORD, have I taken refuge;
let me never be put to shame;
  deliver me in your righteousness.

Incline your ear to me;
  make haste to deliver me.

Be my strong rock, a castle to keep me safe,
for you are my crag and my stronghold;
  for the sake of your Name, lead me and guide me.

Take me out of the net that they have secretly set for me,
  for you are my tower of strength.

Into your hands I commend my spirit,
    for you have redeemed me,
    O Lord, O God of truth.

I hate those who cling to worthless idols,
    and I put my trust in the Lord.

I will rejoice and be glad because of your mercy;
    for you have seen my affliction;
    you know my distress.

You have not shut me up in the power of the enemy;
    you have set my feet in an open place.

Have mercy on me, O Lord, for I am in trouble;
    my eye is consumed with sorrow,
    and also my throat and my belly.

For my life is wasted with grief,
and my years with sighing;
    my strength fails me because of affliction,
    and my bones are consumed.

I have become a reproach to all my enemies and
        even to my neighbors,
a dismay to those of my acquaintance;
    when they see me in the street they avoid me.

I am forgotten like a dead man, out of mind;
    I am as useless as a broken pot.

For I have heard the whispering of the crowd;
fear is all around;
    they put their heads together against me;
    they plot to take my life.

But as for me, I have trusted in you, O Lord.
    I have said, "You are my God.

My times are in your hand;
>   rescue me from the hand of my enemies,
>   and from those who persecute me.

Make your face to shine upon your servant,
>   and in your loving-kindness save me."

LORD, let me not be ashamed for having called upon you;
>   rather, let the wicked be put to shame;
>   let them be silent in the grave.

Let the lying lips be silenced which speak against
>   the righteous,
>   haughtily, disdainfully, and with contempt.

How great is your goodness, O LORD!
which you have laid up for those who fear you;
>   which you have done in the sight of all
>   for those who put their trust in you.

You hide them in the covert of your presence from those
>   who slander them;
>   you keep them in your shelter from the strife of tongues.

Blessed be the LORD!
>   for he has shown me the wonders of his love in a
>   besieged city.

Yet I said in my alarm,
"I have been cut off from the sight of your eyes."
>   Nevertheless, you heard the sound of my entreaty
>   when I cried out to you.

Love the LORD, all you who worship him;
>   the LORD protects the faithful,
>   but repays to the full those who act haughtily.

Be strong and let your heart take courage,
>   all you who wait for the LORD.

⁓ PSALM 52

If you have been slandered before an evil king and you see the devil boasting about it, walk away and say the words in Psalm 52.

You tyrant, why do you boast of wickedness
    against the godly all day long?

You plot ruin;
your tongue is like a sharpened razor,
    O worker of deception.

You love evil more than good
    and lying more than speaking the truth.

You love all words that hurt,
    O you deceitful tongue.

Oh, that God would demolish you utterly,
    topple you, and snatch you from your dwelling,
    and root you out of the land of the living!

The righteous shall see and tremble,
    and they shall laugh at him, saying,

"This is the one who did not take God for a refuge,
    but trusted in great wealth
    and relied upon wickedness."

But I am like a green olive tree in the house of God;
    I trust in the mercy of God for ever and ever.

I will give you thanks for what you have done
    and declare the goodness of your Name in the presence
        of the godly.

PSALMS 54 AND 56

When you are being hounded and certain people slander and seek to betray you, as the Ziphites and foreign tribes did to David, do not despair, but having confidence in the Lord and praising him, say the words in Psalms 54 and 56.

⌒ PSALM 54

Save me, O God, by your Name;
    in your might, defend my cause.

Hear my prayer, O God;
    give ear to the words of my mouth.

For the arrogant have risen up against me,
and the ruthless have sought my life,
    those who have no regard for God.

Behold, God is my helper;
    it is the Lord who sustains my life.

Render evil to those who spy on me;
    in your faithfulness, destroy them.

I will offer you a freewill sacrifice
    and praise your Name, O LORD, for it is good.

For you have rescued me from every trouble,
    and my eye has seen the ruin of my foes.

⌒ PSALM 56

Have mercy on me, O God,
for my enemies are hounding me;
    all day long they assault and oppress me.

They hound me all the day long;
    truly there are many who fight against me, O Most High.

Whenever I am afraid,
  I will put my trust in you.

In God, whose word I praise,
in God I trust and will not be afraid,
  for what can flesh do to me?

All day long they damage my cause;
  their only thought is to do me evil.

They band together; they lie in wait;
  they spy upon my footsteps;
  because they seek my life.

Shall they escape despite their wickedness?
  O God, in your anger, cast down the peoples.

You have noted my lamentation;
put my tears into your bottle;
  are they not recorded in your book?

Whenever I call upon you, my enemies will be put to flight;
  this I know, for God is on my side.

In God the LORD, whose word I praise,
in God I trust and will not be afraid,
  for what can mortals do to me?

I am bound by the vow I made to you, O God;
  I will present to you thank-offerings;

For you have rescued my soul from death and my feet
        from stumbling,
  that I may walk before God in the light of the living.

∽ PSALM 55

When your enemies pressure and mock you, and when people pretending to be friends trick and slander you such that you are nervous in your conversation for awhile, be comforted by praising God and saying the words in Psalm 55.

Hear my prayer, O God;
    do not hide yourself from my petition.

Listen to me and answer me;
    I have no peace, because of my cares.

I am shaken by the noise of the enemy
    and by the pressure of the wicked;

For they have cast an evil spell upon me
    and are set against me in fury.

My heart quakes within me,
    and the terrors of death have fallen upon me.

Fear and trembling have come over me,
    and horror overwhelms me.

And I said, "Oh, that I had wings like a dove!
    I would fly away and be at rest.

I would flee to a far-off place
    and make my lodging in the wilderness.

I would hasten to escape
    from the stormy wind and tempest."

Swallow them up, O Lord;
confound their speech;
    for I have seen violence and strife in the city.

Day and night the watchmen make their rounds upon her walls,
    but trouble and misery are in the midst of her.

There is corruption at her heart;
    her streets are never free of oppression and deceit.

For had it been an adversary who taunted me,
then I could have borne it;
    or had it been an enemy who vaunted himself against me,
    then I could have hidden from him.

But it was you, a man after my own heart,
    my companion, my own familiar friend.

We took sweet counsel together,
    and walked with the throng in the house of God.

Let death come upon them suddenly;
let them go down alive into the grave;
    for wickedness is in their dwellings, in their very midst.

But I will call upon God,
    and the LORD will deliver me.

In the evening, in the morning, and at noonday,
I will complain and lament,
    and he will hear my voice.

He will bring me safely back from the battle
        waged against me;
    for there are many who fight me.

God, who is enthroned of old, will hear me and
        bring them down;
    they never change; they do not fear God.

My companion stretched forth his hand against his comrade;
    he has broken his covenant.

His speech is softer than butter,
    but war is in his heart.

His words are smoother than oil,
  but they are drawn swords.

Cast your burden upon the LORD,
and he will sustain you;
  he will never let the righteous stumble.

For you will bring the bloodthirsty and deceitful
  down to the pit of destruction, O God.

They shall not live out half their days,
  but I will put my trust in you.

PSALMS 57 AND 142

If the person pursuing you overtakes you, and unknowingly enters the
cave in which you are hiding, do not crouch in fear. For in a necessity
such as this you have divine words for comfort and memorial in Psalms
57 and 142.

〜 PSALM 57

Be merciful to me, O God, be merciful,
for I have taken refuge in you;
  in the shadow of your wings will I take refuge
  until this time of trouble has gone by.

I will call upon the Most High God,
  the God who maintains my cause.

He will send from heaven and save me;
he will confound those who trample upon me;
  God will send forth his love and his faithfulness.

I lie in the midst of lions that devour the people;
  their teeth are spears and arrows,
  their tongue a sharp sword.

They have laid a net for my feet,
and I am bowed low;
   they have dug a pit before me,
   but have fallen into it themselves.

Exalt yourself above the heavens, O God,
   and your glory over all the earth.

My heart is firmly fixed, O God, my heart is fixed;
   I will sing and make melody.

Wake up, my spirit;
awake, lute and harp;
   I myself will waken the dawn.

I will confess you among the peoples, O LORD;
   I will sing praise to you among the nations.

For your loving-kindness is greater than the heavens,
   and your faithfulness reaches to the clouds.

Exalt yourself above the heavens, O God,
   and your glory over all the earth.

⌒ PSALM 142

I cry to the LORD with my voice;
   to the LORD I make loud supplication.

I pour out my complaint before him
   and tell him all my trouble.

When my spirit languishes within me, you know my path;
   in the way wherein I walk they have hidden a trap for me.

I look to my right hand and find no one who knows me;
   I have no place to flee to, and no one cares for me.

I cry out to you, O LORD;
>   I say, "You are my refuge,
>   my portion in the land of the living."

Listen to my cry for help, for I have been brought very low;
>   save me from those who pursue me,
>   for they are too strong for me.

Bring me out of prison, that I may give thanks to your Name;
>   when you have dealt bountifully with me,
>   the righteous will gather around me.

⟿ PSALM 59

If the one who is scheming against you gives the order for your house to be guarded closely and you escape, credit the gift to the Lord and mark it on your soul as a memorial of your not being destroyed, and say the words in Psalm 59.

Rescue me from my enemies, O God;
>   protect me from those who rise up against me.

Rescue me from evildoers
>   and save me from those who thirst for my blood.

See how they lie in wait for my life,
how the mighty gather together against me;
>   not for any offense or fault of mine, O LORD.

Not because of any guilt of mine
>   they run and prepare themselves for battle.

Rouse yourself, come to my side, and see;
>   for you, LORD God of hosts, are Israel's God.

Awake, and punish all the ungodly;
>   show no mercy to those who are faithless and evil.

They go to and fro in the evening;
    they snarl like dogs and run about the city.

Behold, they boast with their mouths,
and taunts are on their lips;
    "For who," they say, "will hear us?"

But you, O LORD, you laugh at them;
    you laugh all the ungodly to scorn.

My eyes are fixed on you, O my Strength;
    for you, O God, are my stronghold.

My merciful God comes to meet me;
    God will let me look in triumph on my enemies.

Slay them, O God, lest my people forget;
    send them reeling by your might
    and put them down, O Lord our shield.

For the sins of their mouths, for the words of their lips,
for the cursing and lies that they utter,
    let them be caught in their pride.

Make an end of them in your wrath;
    make an end of them, and they shall be no more.

Let everyone know that God rules in Jacob,
    and to the ends of the earth.

They go to and fro in the evening;
    they snarl like dogs and run about the city.

They forage for food,
    and if they are not filled, they howl.

For my part, I will sing of your strength;
    I will celebrate your love in the morning;

For you have become my stronghold,
    a refuge in the day of my trouble.

To you, O my Strength, will I sing;
    for you, O God, are my stronghold and my merciful God.

◌ PSALM 109

Psalms 2 and 109 indicate the evil plot and wickedness of the Jews as
well as the betrayal by Judas Iscariot.

Hold not your tongue, O God of my praise;
    for the mouth of the wicked,
    the mouth of the deceitful, is opened against me.

They speak to me with a lying tongue;
    they encompass me with hateful words
    and fight against me without a cause.

Despite my love, they accuse me;
    but as for me, I pray for them.

They repay evil for good,
    and hatred for my love.

Set a wicked man against him,
    and let an accuser stand at his right hand.

When he is judged, let him be found guilty,
    and let his appeal be in vain.

Let his days be few,
    and let another take his office.

Let his children be fatherless,
    and his wife become a widow.

Let his children be waifs and beggars;
    let them be driven from the ruins of their homes.

Let the creditor seize everything he has;
    let strangers plunder his gains.

Let there be no one to show him kindness,
    and none to pity his fatherless children.

Let his descendants be destroyed,
    and his name be blotted out in the next generation.

Let the wickedness of his fathers be remembered before
        the LORD,
    and his mother's sin not be blotted out;

Let their sin be always before the LORD;
    but let him root out their names from the earth;

Because he did not remember to show mercy,
    but persecuted the poor and needy
    and sought to kill the brokenhearted.

He loved cursing,
let it come upon him;
    he took no delight in blessing,
    let it depart from him.

He put on cursing like a garment,
    let it soak into his body like water
    and into his bones like oil;

Let it be to him like the cloak which he
        wraps around himself,
    and like the belt that he wears continually.

Let this be the recompense from the LORD to my accusers,
    and to those who speak evil against me.

But you, O Lord my God,
oh, deal with me according to your Name;
    for your tender mercy's sake, deliver me.

For I am poor and needy,
    and my heart is wounded within me.

I have faded away like a shadow when it lengthens;
    I am shaken off like a locust.

My knees are weak through fasting,
    and my flesh is wasted and gaunt.

I have become a reproach to them;
    they see and shake their heads.

Help me, O LORD my God;
    save me for your mercy's sake.

Let them know that this is your hand,
    that you, O LORD, have done it.

They may curse, but you will bless;
    let those who rise up against me be put to shame,
    and your servant will rejoice.

Let my accusers be clothed with disgrace
    and wrap themselves in their shame as in a cloak.

I will give great thanks to the LORD with my mouth;
    in the midst of the multitude will I praise him;

Because he stands at the right hand of the needy,
    to save his life from those who would condemn him.

THREE

Psalms for the Harassed

⟋ PSALM 5

When you see people planning to act maliciously toward you and you want your prayer to be heard, get up at dawn and sing Psalm 5.

Give ear to my words, O LORD;
   consider my meditation.

Hearken to my cry for help, my King and my God,
   for I make my prayer to you.

In the morning, LORD, you hear my voice;
   early in the morning I make my appeal and watch for you.

For you are not a God who takes pleasure in wickedness,
   and evil cannot dwell with you.

Braggarts cannot stand in your sight;
   you hate all those who work wickedness.

You destroy those who speak lies;
   the bloodthirsty and deceitful, O LORD, you abhor.

But as for me, through the greatness of your mercy I will
         go into your house;
   I will bow down toward your holy temple in awe of you.

Lead me, O LORD, in your righteousness,
because of those who lie in wait for me;
   make your way straight before me.

For there is no truth in their mouth;
   there is destruction in their heart;

Their throat is an open grave;
    they flatter with their tongue.

Declare them guilty, O God;
    let them fall, because of their schemes.

Because of their many transgressions cast them out,
    for they have rebelled against you.

But all who take refuge in you will be glad;
    they will sing out their joy for ever.

You will shelter them,
    so that those who love your Name may exult in you.

For you, O LORD, will bless the righteous;
    you will defend them with your favor as with a shield.

ⵢ PSALM 11

Whenever someone delights in harassing you, place your trust in the
Lord, and sing Psalm 11.*

In the LORD have I taken refuge;
    how then can you say to me,
        "Fly away like a bird to the hilltop;

For see how the wicked bend the bow
and fit their arrows to the string,
    to shoot from ambush at the true of heart.

When the foundations are being destroyed,
    what can the righteous do?"

The LORD is in his holy temple;
    the LORD'S throne is in heaven.

His eyes behold the inhabited world;
    his piercing eye weighs our worth.

* Athanasius's LXX version of Psalm 10 corresponds to Psalm 11 in the BCP.

The LORD weighs the righteous as well as the wicked,
  but those who delight in violence he abhors.

Upon the wicked he shall rain coals of fire and
      burning sulphur;
  a scorching wind shall be their lot.

For the LORD is righteous;
he delights in righteous deeds;
  and the just shall see his face.

∾ PSALM 13

If the scheming of your enemies continues for a long time, do not be
discouraged as though God had forgotten you, but appeal to the Lord,
singing Psalm 13.

How long, O LORD?
will you forget me for ever?
  how long will you hide your face from me?

How long shall I have perplexity in my mind,
and grief in my heart, day after day?
  how long shall my enemy triumph over me?

Look upon me and answer me, O LORD my God;
  give light to my eyes, lest I sleep in death;

Lest my enemy say, "I have prevailed over him,"
  and my foes rejoice that I have fallen.

But I put my trust in your mercy;
  my heart is joyful because of your saving help.

I will sing to the LORD, for he has dealt with me richly;
  I will praise the Name of the Lord Most High.

PSALMS 17, 86, 88, AND 141

When you need prayer because those set against you are surrounding you, threatening your life, sing Psalms 17, 86, 88, and 141.

∽ PSALM 17

Hear my plea of innocence, O LORD;
give heed to my cry;
listen to my prayer, which does not come from lying lips.

Let my vindication come forth from your presence;
let your eyes be fixed on justice.

Weigh my heart, summon me by night,
melt me down; you will find no impurity in me.

I give no offense with my mouth as others do;
I have heeded the words of your lips.

My footsteps hold fast to the ways of your law;
in your paths my feet shall not stumble.

I call upon you, O God, for you will answer me;
incline your ear to me and hear my words.

Show me your marvelous loving-kindness,
O Savior of those who take refuge at your right hand
from those who rise up against them.

Keep me as the apple of your eye;
hide me under the shadow of your wings,

From the wicked who assault me,
from my deadly enemies who surround me.

They have closed their heart to pity,
and their mouth speaks proud things.

They press me hard,
now they surround me,
    watching how they may cast me to the ground,

Like a lion, greedy for its prey,
    and like a young lion lurking in secret places.

Arise, O LORD; confront them and bring them down;
    deliver me from the wicked by your sword.

Deliver me, O LORD, by your hand
    from those whose portion in life is this world;

Whose bellies you fill with your treasure,
    who are well supplied with children
    and leave their wealth to their little ones.

But at my vindication I shall see your face;
    when I awake, I shall be satisfied, beholding
        your likeness.

⌒ PSALM 86

Bow down your ear, O LORD, and answer me,
    for I am poor and in misery.

Keep watch over my life, for I am faithful;
    save your servant who puts his trust in you.

Be merciful to me, O LORD, for you are my God;
    I call upon you all the day long.

Gladden the soul of your servant,
    for to you, O LORD, I lift up my soul.

For you, O LORD, are good and forgiving,
    and great is your love toward all who call upon you.

Give ear, O LORD, to my prayer,
    and attend to the voice of my supplications.

In the time of my trouble I will call upon you,
    for you will answer me.

Among the gods there is none like you, O LORD,
    nor anything like your works.

All nations you have made will come and
                worship you, O LORD,
    and glorify your Name.

For you are great;
you do wondrous things;
    and you alone are God.

Teach me your way, O LORD,
and I will walk in your truth;
    knit my heart to you that I may fear your Name.

I will thank you, O LORD my God, with all my heart,
    and glorify your Name for evermore.

For great is your love toward me;
    you have delivered me from the nethermost Pit.

The arrogant rise up against me, O God,
and a band of violent men seeks my life;
    they have not set you before their eyes.

But you, O LORD, are gracious and full of compassion,
    slow to anger, and full of kindness and truth.

Turn to me and have mercy upon me;
    give your strength to your servant;
    and save the child of your handmaid.

Show me a sign of your favor,
so that those who hate me may see it and be ashamed;
    because you, O LORD, have helped me and comforted me.

☙ PSALM 88

O LORD, my God, my Savior,
    by day and night I cry to you.

Let my prayer enter into your presence;
    incline your ear to my lamentation.

For I am full of trouble;
    my life is at the brink of the grave.

I am counted among those who go down to the Pit;
    I have become like one who has no strength;

Lost among the dead,
    like the slain who lie in the grave,

Whom you remember no more,
    for they are cut off from your hand.

You have laid me in the depths of the Pit,
    in dark places, and in the abyss.

Your anger weighs upon me heavily,
    and all your great waves overwhelm me.

You have put my friends far from me;
you have made me to be abhorred by them;
    I am in prison and cannot get free.

My sight has failed me because of trouble;
    LORD, I have called upon you daily;
    I have stretched out my hands to you.

Do you work wonders for the dead?
    will those who have died stand up and give you thanks?

Will your loving-kindness be declared in the grave?
    your faithfulness in the land of destruction?

Will your wonders be known in the dark?
    or your righteousness in the country where all
        is forgotten?

But as for me, O LORD, I cry to you for help;
    in the morning my prayer comes before you.

LORD, why have you rejected me?
    why have you hidden your face from me?

Ever since my youth, I have been wretched and at the
        point of death;
    I have borne your terrors with a troubled mind.

Your blazing anger has swept over me;
    your terrors have destroyed me;

They surround me all day long like a flood;
    they encompass me on every side.

My friend and my neighbor you have put away from me,
    and darkness is my only companion.

∿ PSALM 141

O LORD, I call to you; come to me quickly;
    hear my voice when I cry to you.

Let my prayer be set forth in your sight as incense,
    the lifting up of my hands as the evening sacrifice.

Set a watch before my mouth, O LORD,
and guard the door of my lips;
    let not my heart incline to any evil thing.

Let me not be occupied in wickedness with evildoers,
    nor eat of their choice foods.

Let the righteous smite me in friendly rebuke;
let not the oil of the unrighteous anoint my head;
    for my prayer is continually against their wicked deeds.

Let their rulers be overthrown in stony places,
    that they may know my words are true.

As when a plowman turns over the earth in furrows,
    let their bones be scattered at the mouth of the grave.

But my eyes are turned to you, Lord GOD;
    in you I take refuge;
    do not strip me of my life.

Protect me from the snare which they have laid for me
    and from the traps of the evildoers.

Let the wicked fall into their own nets,
        while I myself escape.

➴ PSALM 25

When your enemies surround you, nevertheless lift up your soul to God
and say Psalm 25, and you will see them fail in their wicked schemes.

To you, O LORD, I lift up my soul;
my God, I put my trust in you;
    let me not be humiliated,
    nor let my enemies triumph over me.

Let none who look to you be put to shame;
    let the treacherous be disappointed in their schemes.

Show me your ways, O LORD,
    and teach me your paths.

Lead me in your truth and teach me,
    for you are the God of my salvation;
    in you have I trusted all the day long.

Remember, O LORD, your compassion and love,
   for they are from everlasting.

Remember not the sins of my youth and my transgressions;
   remember me according to your love
   and for the sake of your goodness, O LORD.

Gracious and upright is the LORD;
   therefore he teaches sinners in his way.

He guides the humble in doing right
   and teaches his way to the lowly.

All the paths of the LORD are love and faithfulness
   to those who keep his covenant and his testimonies.

For your Name's sake, O LORD,
   forgive my sin, for it is great.

Who are they who fear the LORD?
   he will teach them the way that they should choose.

They shall dwell in prosperity,
   and their offspring shall inherit the land.

The LORD is a friend to those who fear him
   and will show them his covenant.

My eyes are ever looking to the LORD,
   for he shall pluck my feet out of the net.

Turn to me and have pity on me,
   for I am left alone and in misery.

The sorrows of my heart have increased;
   bring me out of my troubles.

Look upon my adversity and misery
   and forgive me all my sin.

Look upon my enemies, for they are many,
   and they bear a violent hatred against me.

Protect my life and deliver me;
    let me not be put to shame, for I have trusted in you.

Let integrity and uprightness preserve me,
    for my hope has been in you.

Deliver Israel, O God,
    out of all his troubles.

PSALMS 26, 35, AND 43

But if your enemies remain, having nothing other than hands full of blood, and they are intending to drag you down and destroy you, do not entrust the judgment to a man (for everything human is dubious), but regarding God to be the judge (for he alone is just), say the words of Psalms 26, 35, and 43.

∾ PSALM 26

Give judgment for me, O LORD,
for I have lived with integrity;
    I have trusted in the Lord and have not faltered.

Test me, O LORD, and try me;
    examine my heart and my mind.

For your love is before my eyes;
    I have walked faithfully with you.

I have not sat with the worthless,
    nor do I consort with the deceitful.

I have hated the company of evildoers;
    I will not sit down with the wicked.

I will wash my hands in innocence, O LORD,
    that I may go in procession round your altar,

Singing aloud a song of thanksgiving
    and recounting all your wonderful deeds.

LORD, I love the house in which you dwell
    and the place where your glory abides.

Do not sweep me away with sinners,
    nor my life with those who thirst for blood,

Whose hands are full of evil plots,
    and their right hand full of bribes.

As for me, I will live with integrity;
    redeem me, O LORD, and have pity on me.

My foot stands on level ground;
    in the full assembly I will bless the LORD.

∾ PSALM 35

Fight those who fight me, O LORD;
    attack those who are attacking me.

Take up shield and armor
    and rise up to help me.

Draw the sword and bar the way against those
            who pursue me;
    say to my soul, "I am your salvation."

Let those who seek after my life be shamed and humbled;
    let those who plot my ruin fall back and be dismayed.

Let them be like chaff before the wind,
    and let the angel of the LORD drive them away.

Let their way be dark and slippery,
    and let the angel of the LORD pursue them.

For they have secretly spread a net for me without a cause;
  without a cause they have dug a pit to take me alive.

Let ruin come upon them unawares;
  let them be caught in the net they hid;
  let them fall into the pit they dug.

Then I will be joyful in the LORD;
  I will glory in his victory.

My very bones will say, "LORD, who is like you?
  You deliver the poor from those who are too strong for them,
  the poor and needy from those who rob them."

Malicious witnesses rise up against me;
  they charge me with matters I know nothing about.

They pay me evil in exchange for good;
  my soul is full of despair.

But when they were sick I dressed in sack-cloth
  and humbled myself by fasting;

I prayed with my whole heart,
as one would for a friend or a brother;
  I behaved like one who mourns for his mother,
  bowed down and grieving.

But when I stumbled, they were glad and gathered together;
they gathered against me;
  strangers whom I did not know tore me to pieces and
       would not stop.

They put me to the test and mocked me;
  they gnashed at me with their teeth.

O Lord, how long will you look on?
  rescue me from the roaring beasts,
  and my life from the young lions.

I will give you thanks in the great congregation;
    I will praise you in the mighty throng.

Do not let my treacherous foes rejoice over me,
    nor let those who hate me without a cause
        wink at each other.

For they do not plan for peace,
    but invent deceitful schemes against the
        quiet in the land.

They opened their mouths at me and said,
    "Aha! we saw it with our own eyes."

You saw it, O LORD; do not be silent;
    O Lord, be not far from me.

Awake, arise, to my cause!
    to my defense, my God and my Lord!

Give me justice, O LORD my God,
according to your righteousness;
    do not let them triumph over me.

Do not let them say in their hearts,
"Aha! just what we want!"
    Do not let them say, "We have swallowed him up."

Let all who rejoice at my ruin be ashamed and disgraced;
    let those who boast against me be clothed with
        dismay and shame.

Let those who favor my cause sing out with joy and be glad;
    let them say always, "Great is the LORD,
    who desires the prosperity of his servant."

And my tongue shall be talking of your righteousness
    and of your praise all the day long.

⌒ PSALM 43

Give judgment for me, O God,
and defend my cause against an ungodly people;
    deliver me from the deceitful and the wicked.

For you are the God of my strength;
why have you put me from you?
    and why do I go so heavily while the enemy
        oppresses me?

Send out your light and your truth, that they may lead me,
    and bring me to your holy hill
    and to your dwelling;

That I may go to the altar of God,
to the God of my joy and gladness;
    and on the harp I will give thanks to you, O God my God.

Why are you so full of heaviness, O my soul?
    and why are you so disquieted within me?

Put your trust in God;
    for I will yet give thanks to him,
    who is the help of my countenance, and my God.

⌒ PSALM 37

When you see wicked people who frequently disregard the law and rise up against smaller people, and you want to convince the latter not to join them or be jealous of them since such people quickly fade away, then say to yourself and to the others Psalm 37.

Do not fret yourself because of evildoers;
    do not be jealous of those who do wrong.

For they shall soon wither like the grass,
    and like the green grass fade away.

Put your trust in the LORD and do good;
  dwell in the land and feed on its riches.

Take delight in the LORD,
  and he shall give you your heart's desire.

Commit your way to the LORD and put your trust in him,
  and he will bring it to pass.

He will make your righteousness as clear as the light
  and your just dealing as the noonday.

Be still before the Lord
  and wait patiently for him.

Do not fret yourself over the one who prospers,
  the one who succeeds in evil schemes.

Refrain from anger, leave rage alone;
  do not fret yourself; it leads only to evil.

For evildoers shall be cut off,
  but those who wait upon the LORD shall possess the land.

In a little while the wicked shall be no more;
  you shall search out their place, but they will not be there.

But the lowly shall possess the land;
  they will delight in abundance of peace.

The wicked plot against the righteous
  and gnash at them with their teeth.

The Lord laughs at the wicked,
  because he sees that their day will come.

The wicked draw their sword and bend their bow
to strike down the poor and needy,
  to slaughter those who are upright in their ways.

Their sword shall go through their own heart,
   and their bow shall be broken.

The little that the righteous has
   is better than great riches of the wicked.

For the power of the wicked shall be broken,
   but the LORD upholds the righteous.

The LORD cares for the lives of the godly,
   and their inheritance shall last for ever.

They shall not be ashamed in bad times,
   and in days of famine they shall have enough.

As for the wicked, they shall perish,
   and the enemies of the LORD, like the glory of
      the meadows, shall vanish;
   they shall vanish like smoke.

The wicked borrow and do not repay,
   but the righteous are generous in giving.

Those who are blessed by God shall possess the land,
   but those who are cursed by him shall be destroyed.

Our steps are directed by the LORD;
   he strengthens those in whose way he delights.

If they stumble, they shall not fall headlong,
   for the LORD holds them by the hand.

I have been young and now I am old,
   but never have I seen the righteous forsaken,
   or their children begging bread.

The righteous are always generous in their lending,
   and their children shall be a blessing.

Turn from evil, and do good,
    and dwell in the land for ever.

For the LORD loves justice;
    he does not forsake his faithful ones.

They shall be kept safe for ever,
    but the offspring of the wicked shall be destroyed.

The righteous shall possess the land
    and dwell in it for ever.

The mouth of the righteous utters wisdom,
    and their tongue speaks what is right.

The law of their God is in their heart,
    and their footsteps shall not falter.

The wicked spy on the righteous
    and seek occasion to kill them.

The LORD will not abandon them to their hand,
    nor let them be found guilty when brought to trial.

Wait upon the LORD and keep his way;
    he will raise you up to possess the land,
    and when the wicked are cut off, you will see it.

I have seen the wicked in their arrogance,
    flourishing like a tree in full leaf.

I went by, and behold, they were not there;
    I searched for them, but they could not be found.

Mark those who are honest;
observe the upright;
    for there is a future for the peaceable.

Transgressors shall be destroyed, one and all;
    the future of the wicked is cut off.

But the deliverance of the righteous comes from the LORD;
  he is their stronghold in time of trouble.

The LORD will help them and rescue them;
  he will rescue them from the wicked and deliver them,
  because they seek refuge in him.

⌐ PSALM 39

If you are in need and want to pray on your own behalf as you see your
enemy closing in—for at that time one has good reason to be on guard
against such people—and you want to arm yourself against him, sing
Psalm 39.

I said, "I will keep watch upon my ways,
  so that I do not offend with my tongue.

I will put a muzzle on my mouth
  while the wicked are in my presence."

So I held my tongue and said nothing;
  I refrained from rash words;
  but my pain became unbearable.

My heart was hot within me;
while I pondered, the fire burst into flame;
  I spoke out with my tongue:

LORD, let me know my end and the number of my days,
  so that I may know how short my life is.

You have given me a mere handful of days,
and my lifetime is as nothing in your sight;
  truly, even those who stand erect are but a puff of wind.

We walk about like a shadow,
and in vain we are in turmoil;
  we heap up riches and cannot tell who will gather them.

And now, what is my hope?
O Lord, my hope is in you.

Deliver me from all my transgressions
and do not make me the taunt of the fool.

I fell silent and did not open my mouth,
for surely it was you that did it.

Take your affliction from me;
I am worn down by the blows of your hand.

With rebukes for sin you punish us;
like a moth you eat away all that is dear to us;
truly, everyone is but a puff of wind.

Hear my prayer, O LORD,
and give ear to my cry;
hold not your peace at my tears.

For I am but a sojourner with you,
a wayfarer, as all my forebears were.

Turn your gaze from me, that I may be glad again,
before I go my way and am no more.

～ PSALM 62

When people violently attack you and try to take your life, surrender to God and take courage. However much they rage, so much more should you surrender to the Lord and say the words in Psalm 62.

For God alone my soul in silence waits;
from him comes my salvation.

He alone is my rock and my salvation,
my stronghold, so that I shall not be greatly shaken.

How long will you assail me to crush me,
all of you together,
   as if you were a leaning fence, a toppling wall?

They seek only to bring me down from my place of honor;
   lies are their chief delight.

They bless with their lips,
   but in their hearts they curse.

For God alone my soul in silence waits;
   truly, my hope is in him.

He alone is my rock and my salvation,
   my stronghold, so that I shall not be shaken.

In God is my safety and my honor;
   God is my strong rock and my refuge.

Put your trust in him always, O people,
   pour out your hearts before him, for God is our refuge.

Those of high degree are but a fleeting breath,
   even those of low estate cannot be trusted.

On the scales they are lighter than a breath,
   all of them together.

Put no trust in extortion;
in robbery take no empty pride;
   though wealth increase, set not your heart upon it.

God has spoken once, twice have I heard it,
   that power belongs to God.

Steadfast love is yours, O Lord,
   for you repay everyone according to his deeds.

๑ PSALM 63

If when you are harassed you run to the desert, do not be afraid as
though you are alone there. But having God there, get up at dawn and
sing to him Psalm 63.

O God, you are my God; eagerly I seek you;
 my soul thirsts for you, my flesh faints for you,
  as in a barren and dry land where there is no water.

Therefore I have gazed upon you in your holy place,
 that I might behold your power and your glory.

For your loving-kindness is better than life itself;
 my lips shall give you praise.

So will I bless you as long as I live
 and lift up my hands in your Name.

My soul is content, as with marrow and fatness,
 and my mouth praises you with joyful lips,

When I remember you upon my bed,
 and meditate on you in the night watches.

For you have been my helper,
 and under the shadow of your wings I will rejoice.

My soul clings to you;
 your right hand holds me fast.

May those who seek my life to destroy it
 go down into the depths of the earth;

Let them fall upon the edge of the sword,
 and let them be food for jackals.

But the king will rejoice in God;
all those who swear by him will be glad;
 for the mouth of those who speak lies shall be stopped.

PSALMS 64, 70, AND 71

If you are afraid of your enemies who do not stop trying to ambush you and search everywhere for you, even if they are numerous, do not give in. For when you sing Psalms 64, 65, 70, and 71, their arrows will be like the toy darts of childhood.

✎ PSALM 64

Hear my voice, O God, when I complain;
 protect my life from fear of the enemy.

Hide me from the conspiracy of the wicked,
 from the mob of evildoers.

They sharpen their tongue like a sword,
 and aim their bitter words like arrows,

That they may shoot down the blameless from ambush;
 they shoot without warning and are not afraid.

They hold fast to their evil course;
 they plan how they may hide their snares.

They say, "Who will see us?
who will find out our crimes?
 we have thought out a perfect plot."

The human mind and heart are a mystery;
 but God will loose an arrow at them,
 and suddenly they will be wounded.

He will make them trip over their tongues,
 and all who see them will shake their heads.

Everyone will stand in awe and declare God's deeds;
 they will recognize his works.

The righteous will rejoice in the LORD and put their trust in him,
 and all who are true of heart will glory.

∽ PSALM 70

Be pleased, O God, to deliver me;
  O Lord, make haste to help me.

Let those who seek my life be ashamed
and altogether dismayed;
  let those who take pleasure in my misfortune
  draw back and be disgraced.

Let those who say to me "Aha!" and gloat over me turn back,
  because they are ashamed.

Let all who seek you rejoice and be glad in you;
  let those who love your salvation say for ever,
  "Great is the Lord!"

But as for me, I am poor and needy;
  come to me speedily, O God.

You are my helper and my deliverer;
  O Lord, do not tarry.

∽ PSALM 71

In you, O Lord, have I taken refuge;
  let me never be ashamed.

In your righteousness, deliver me and set me free;
  incline your ear to me and save me.

Be my strong rock, a castle to keep me safe;
  you are my crag and my stronghold.

Deliver me, my God, from the hand of the wicked,
  from the clutches of the evildoer and the oppressor.

For you are my hope, O Lord God,
  my confidence since I was young.

I have been sustained by you ever since I was born;
from my mother's womb you have been my strength;
   my praise shall be always of you.

I have become a portent to many;
   but you are my refuge and my strength.

Let my mouth be full of your praise
 and your glory all the day long.

Do not cast me off in my old age;
   forsake me not when my strength fails.

For my enemies are talking against me,
   and those who lie in wait for my life take counsel together.

They say, "God has forsaken him;
go after him and seize him;
   because there is none who will save."

O God, be not far from me;
   come quickly to help me, O my God.

Let those who set themselves against me be put to shame and
            be disgraced;
   let those who seek to do me evil be covered with scorn
            and reproach.

But I shall always wait in patience,
   and shall praise you more and more.

My mouth shall recount your mighty acts
and saving deeds all day long;
   though I cannot know the number of them.

I will begin with the mighty works of the Lord GOD;
   I will recall your righteousness, yours alone.

O God, you have taught me since I was young,
   and to this day I tell of your wonderful works.

And now that I am old and gray-headed, O God, do not
        forsake me,
    till I make known your strength to this generation
    and your power to all who are to come.

Your righteousness, O God, reaches to the heavens;
    you have done great things;
    who is like you, O God?

You have showed me great troubles and adversities,
    but you will restore my life
    and bring me up again from the deep places of the earth.

You strengthen me more and more;
    you enfold and comfort me,

Therefore I will praise you upon the lyre for your
        faithfulness, O my God;
    I will sing to you with the harp, O Holy One of Israel.

My lips will sing with joy when I play to you,
    and so will my soul, which you have redeemed.

My tongue will proclaim your righteousness all day long,
    for they are ashamed and disgraced who sought
        to do me harm.

⌒ PSALM 77

When your enemies take over your safe places and you are being harassed everywhere, do not be troubled, but pray. And if when you are
crying out you are heard, thank God by saying the words in Psalm 77.

I will cry aloud to God;
    I will cry aloud, and he will hear me.

In the day of my trouble I sought the Lord;
    my hands were stretched out by night and did not tire;
    I refused to be comforted.

I think of God, I am restless,
 I ponder, and my spirit faints.

You will not let my eyelids close;
 I am troubled and I cannot speak.

I consider the days of old;
 I remember the years long past;

I commune with my heart in the night;
 I ponder and search my mind.

Will the Lord cast me off for ever?
 will he no more show his favor?

Has his loving-kindness come to an end for ever?
 has his promise failed for evermore?

Has God forgotten to be gracious?
 has he, in his anger, withheld his compassion?

And I said, "My grief is this:
 the right hand of the Most High has lost its power."

I will remember the works of the LORD,
 and call to mind your wonders of old time.

I will meditate on all your acts
 and ponder your mighty deeds.

Your way, O God, is holy;
 who is so great a god as our God?

You are the God who works wonders
 and have declared your power among the peoples.

By your strength you have redeemed your people,
 the children of Jacob and Joseph.

The waters saw you, O God;
the waters saw you and trembled;
 the very depths were shaken.

The clouds poured out water;
the skies thundered;
   your arrows flashed to and fro;

The sound of your thunder was in the whirlwind;
your lightnings lit up the world;
   the earth trembled and shook.

Your way was in the sea,
and your paths in the great waters,
   yet your footsteps were not seen.

You led your people like a flock
   by the hand of Moses and Aaron.

～ PSALM 83

When all of your enemies surround you from every side, bringing
threats against the house of God and forming alliances against the
God-fearing, so that you may not lose heart on account of their great
number and power, you have as an anchor of hope the words in
Psalm 83.

O God, do not be silent;
   do not keep still nor hold your peace, O God;

For your enemies are in tumult,
   and those who hate you have lifted up their heads.

They take secret counsel against your people
   and plot against those whom you protect.

They have said, "Come, let us wipe them out from among
       the nations;
   let the name of Israel be remembered no more."

They have conspired together;
   they have made an alliance against you:

The tents of Edom and the Ishmaelites;
　　the Moabites and the Hagarenes;

Gebal, and Ammon, and Amalek;
　　the Philistines and those who dwell in Tyre.

The Assyrians also have joined them,
　　and have come to help the people of Lot.

Do to them as you did to Midian,
　　to Sisera, and to Jabin at the river of Kishon:

They were destroyed at Endor;
　　they became like dung upon the ground.

Make their leaders like Oreb and Zeëb,
　　and all their commanders like Zebah and Zalmunna,

Who said, "Let us take for ourselves
　　the fields of God as our possession."

O my God, make them like whirling dust
　　and like chaff before the wind;

Like fire that burns down a forest,
　　like the flame that sets mountains ablaze.

Drive them with your tempest
　　and terrify them with your storm;

Cover their faces with shame, O LORD,
　　that they may seek your Name.

Let them be disgraced and terrified for ever;
　　let them be put to confusion and perish.

Let them know that you, whose Name is YAHWEH,
　　　　you alone are the Most High over all the earth.

⌒ PSALM 140

Are you surrounded again by enemies and want to be rescued? Say
the words in Psalm 140.

Deliver me, O LORD, from evildoers;
    protect me from the violent,

Who devise evil in their hearts
    and stir up strife all day long.

They have sharpened their tongues like a serpent;
    adder's poison is under their lips.

Keep me, O LORD, from the hands of the wicked;
    protect me from the violent,
    who are determined to trip me up.

The proud have hidden a snare for me
and stretched out a net of cords;
    they have set traps for me along the path.

I have said to the LORD, "You are my God;
    listen, O LORD, to my supplication.

O Lord GOD, the strength of my salvation,
    you have covered my head in the day of battle.

Do not grant the desires of the wicked, O LORD,
    nor let their evil plans prosper.

Let not those who surround me lift up their heads;
    let the evil of their lips overwhelm them.

Let hot burning coals fall upon them;
    let them be cast into the mire, never to rise up again."

A slanderer shall not be established on the earth,
    and evil shall hunt down the lawless.

I know that the LORD will maintain the cause of the poor
and render justice to the needy.

Surely, the righteous will give thanks to your Name,
and the upright shall continue in your sight.

✑ PSALM 144

When a hostile tyrant rises up against the people and you, like Goliath
against David, do not crouch in fear. But have trust like David, and say
the words in Psalm 144.

Blessed be the LORD my rock!
who trains my hands to fight and my fingers to battle;

My help and my fortress, my stronghold and my deliverer,
my shield in whom I trust,
who subdues the peoples under me.

O LORD, what are we that you should care for us?
mere mortals that you should think of us?

We are like a puff of wind;
our days are like a passing shadow.

Bow your heavens, O LORD, and come down;
touch the mountains, and they shall smoke.

Hurl the lightning and scatter them;
shoot out your arrows and rout them.

Stretch out your hand from on high;
rescue me and deliver me from the great waters,
from the hand of foreign peoples,

Whose mouths speak deceitfully
and whose right hand is raised in falsehood.

O God, I will sing to you a new song;
    I will play to you on a ten-stringed lyre.

You give victory to kings
    and have rescued David your servant.

Rescue me from the hurtful sword
    and deliver me from the hand of foreign peoples,

Whose mouths speak deceitfully
    and whose right hand is raised in falsehood.

May our sons be like plants well nurtured from their youth,
    and our daughters like sculptured corners of a palace.

May our barns be filled to overflowing with all manner
            of crops;
    may the flocks in our pastures increase by thousands
            and tens of thousands;
    may our cattle be fat and sleek.

May there be no breaching of the walls, no going into exile,
    no wailing in the public squares.

Happy are the people of whom this is so!
    happy are the people whose God is the LORD!

FOUR

Psalms for the Guilty

PSALMS 6 AND 38

When you feel the disapproval of the Lord and you see that you are troubled by this, you can say Psalms 6 and 38.

ꙅ PSALM 6

LORD, do not rebuke me in your anger;
   do not punish me in your wrath.

Have pity on me, LORD, for I am weak;
   heal me, LORD, for my bones are racked.

My spirit shakes with terror;
   how long, O LORD, how long?

Turn, O LORD, and deliver me;
   save me for your mercy's sake.

For in death no one remembers you;
   and who will give you thanks in the grave?

I grow weary because of my groaning;
   every night I drench my bed
   and flood my couch with tears.

My eyes are wasted with grief
   and worn away because of all my enemies.

Depart from me, all evildoers,
   for the LORD has heard the sound of my weeping.

The LORD has heard my supplication;
  the LORD accepts my prayer.

All my enemies shall be confounded and quake with fear;
  they shall turn back and suddenly be put to shame.

⌾ PSALM 38

O LORD, do not rebuke me in your anger;
  do not punish me in your wrath.

For your arrows have already pierced me,
  and your hand presses hard upon me.

There is no health in my flesh,
because of your indignation;
  there is no soundness in my body, because of my sin.

For my iniquities overwhelm me;
  like a heavy burden they are too much for me to bear.

My wounds stink and fester
  by reason of my foolishness.

I am utterly bowed down and prostrate;
  I go about in mourning all the day long.

My loins are filled with searing pain;
  there is no health in my body.

I am utterly numb and crushed;
  I wail, because of the groaning of my heart.

O Lord, you know all my desires,
  and my sighing is not hidden from you.

My heart is pounding, my strength has failed me,
  and the brightness of my eyes is gone from me.

My friends and companions draw back from my affliction;
    my neighbors stand afar off.

Those who seek after my life lay snares for me;
    those who strive to hurt me speak of my ruin
    and plot treachery all the day long.

But I am like the deaf who do not hear,
    like those who are mute and do not open their mouth.

I have become like one who does not hear
    and from whose mouth comes no defense.

For in you, O LORD, have I fixed my hope;
    you will answer me, O Lord my God.

For I said, "Do not let them rejoice at my expense,
    those who gloat over me when my foot slips."

Truly, I am on the verge of falling,
    and my pain is always with me.

I will confess my iniquity
    and be sorry for my sin.

Those who are my enemies without cause are mighty,
    and many in number are those who wrongfully hate me.

Those who repay evil for good slander me,
    because I follow the course that is right.

O LORD, do not forsake me;
    be not far from me, O my God.

Make haste to help me,
    O Lord of my salvation.

PSALMS 14 AND 53

Whenever you hear people speaking profanely against Providence, do not join them in their disregard for God, but intercede with God, saying Psalms 14 and 53.

～ PSALM 14

The fool has said in his heart, "There is no God."
   All are corrupt and commit abominable acts;
   there is none who does any good.

The LORD looks down from heaven upon us all,
   to see if there is any who is wise,
   if there is one who seeks after God.

Every one has proved faithless;
all alike have turned bad;
   there is none who does good; no, not one.

Have they no knowledge, all those evildoers
   who eat up my people like bread
   and do not call upon the LORD?

See how they tremble with fear,
   because God is in the company of the righteous.

Their aim is to confound the plans of the afflicted,
   but the LORD is their refuge.

Oh, that Israel's deliverance would come out of Zion!
   when the LORD restores the fortunes of his people,
   Jacob will rejoice and Israel be glad.

～ PSALM 53

The fool has said in his heart, "There is no God."
   All are corrupt and commit abominable acts;
   there is none who does any good.

God looks down from heaven upon us all,
  to see if there is any who is wise,
  if there is one who seeks after God.

Every one has proved faithless;
all alike have turned bad;
  there is none who does good; no, not one.

Have they no knowledge, those evildoers
  who eat up my people like bread
  and do not call upon God?

See how greatly they tremble,
such trembling as never was;
  for God has scattered the bones of the enemy;
  they are put to shame, because God has rejected them.

Oh, that Israel's deliverance would come out of Zion!
  when God restores the fortunes of his people
  Jacob will rejoice and Israel be glad.

～ PSALM 51

You sinned and feeling guilty, you repent and ask to be shown mercy.
You have words of confession and conversion in Psalm 51.

Have mercy on me, O God, according to your
          loving-kindness;
  in your great compassion blot out my offenses.

Wash me through and through from my wickedness
  and cleanse me from my sin.

For I know my transgressions,
  and my sin is ever before me.

Against you only have I sinned
  and done what is evil in your sight.

And so you are justified when you speak
and upright in your judgment.

Indeed, I have been wicked from my birth,
a sinner from my mother's womb.

For behold, you look for truth deep within me,
and will make me understand wisdom secretly.

Purge me from my sin, and I shall be pure;
wash me, and I shall be clean indeed.

Make me hear of joy and gladness,
that the body you have broken may rejoice.

Hide your face from my sins
and blot out all my iniquities.

Create in me a clean heart, O God,
and renew a right spirit within me.

Cast me not away from your presence
and take not your holy Spirit from me.

Give me the joy of your saving help again
and sustain me with your bountiful Spirit.

I shall teach your ways to the wicked,
and sinners shall return to you.

Deliver me from death, O God,
and my tongue shall sing of your righteousness,
O God of my salvation.

Open my lips, O Lord,
and my mouth shall proclaim your praise.

Had you desired it, I would have offered sacrifice,
but you take no delight in burnt-offerings.

The sacrifice of God is a troubled spirit;
    a broken and contrite heart, O God, you will not despise.

Be favorable and gracious to Zion,
    and rebuild the walls of Jerusalem.

Then you will be pleased with the appointed sacrifices,
with burnt-offerings and oblations;
    then shall they offer young bullocks upon your altar.

⌃ PSALM 58

Against hypocrites and those who boast about themselves, say Psalm 58 for their correction.

Do you indeed decree righteousness, you rulers?
    do you judge the peoples with equity?

No; you devise evil in your hearts,
    and your hands deal out violence in the land.

The wicked are perverse from the womb;
    liars go astray from their birth.

They are as venomous as a serpent,
    they are like the deaf adder which stops its ears,

Which does not heed the voice of the charmer,
    no matter how skillful his charming.

O God, break their teeth in their mouths;
    pull the fangs of the young lions, O LORD.

Let them vanish like water that runs off;
    let them wither like trodden grass.

Let them be like the snail that melts away,
    like a stillborn child that never sees the sun.

Before they bear fruit, let them be cut down like a brier;
    like thorns and thistles let them be swept away.

The righteous will be glad when they see the vengeance;
    they will bathe their feet in the blood of the wicked.

And they will say,
"Surely, there is a reward for the righteous;
    surely, there is a God who rules in the earth."

⌣ PSALM 67

When you ask for mercy from God, praise him while singing Psalm 67.

May God be merciful to us and bless us,
    show us the light of his countenance and come to us.

Let your ways be known upon earth,
    your saving health among all nations.

Let the peoples praise you, O God;
    let all the peoples praise you.

Let the nations be glad and sing for joy,
    for you judge the peoples with equity
    and guide all the nations upon earth.

Let the peoples praise you, O God;
    let all the peoples praise you.

The earth has brought forth her increase;
    may God, our own God, give us his blessing.

May God give us his blessing,
    and may all the ends of the earth stand in awe of him.

∾ PSALM 74

Whenever God is angry at the community, for comfort in this situation
you have the wise words of Psalm 74.

O God, why have you utterly cast us off?
why is your wrath so hot against the sheep of your pasture?

Remember your congregation that you purchased long ago,
the tribe you redeemed to be your inheritance,
and Mount Zion where you dwell.

Turn your steps toward the endless ruins;
the enemy has laid waste everything in your sanctuary.

Your adversaries roared in your holy place;
they set up their banners as tokens of victory.

They were like men coming up with axes to a grove of trees;
they broke down all your carved work with hatchets
and hammers.

They set fire to your holy place;
they defiled the dwelling-place of your Name
and razed it to the ground.

They said to themselves, "Let us destroy them altogether."
They burned down all the meeting-places of God
in the land.

There are no signs for us to see;
there is no prophet left;
there is not one among us who knows how long.

How long, O God, will the adversary scoff?
will the enemy blaspheme your Name for ever?

Why do you draw back your hand?
why is your right hand hidden in your bosom?

Yet God is my King from ancient times,
    victorious in the midst of the earth.

You divided the sea by your might
    and shattered the heads of the dragons upon the waters;

You crushed the heads of Leviathan
    and gave him to the people of the desert for food.

You split open spring and torrent;
    you dried up ever-flowing rivers.

Yours is the day, yours also the night;
    you established the moon and the sun.

You fixed all the boundaries of the earth;
    you made both summer and winter.

Remember, O LORD, how the enemy scoffed,
    how a foolish people despised your Name.

Do not hand over the life of your dove to wild beasts;
    never forget the lives of your poor.

Look upon your covenant;
    the dark places of the earth are haunts of violence.

Let not the oppressed turn away ashamed;
    let the poor and needy praise your Name.

Arise, O God, maintain your cause;
    remember how fools revile you all day long.

Forget not the clamor of your adversaries,
    the unending tumult of those who rise up against you.

◯ PSALM 82

Psalms 58 and 82 awaken one's guilt.

God takes his stand in the council of heaven;
    he gives judgment in the midst of the gods:

"How long will you judge unjustly,
    and show favor to the wicked?

Save the weak and the orphan;
    defend the humble and needy;

Rescue the weak and the poor;
    deliver them from the power of the wicked.

They do not know, neither do they understand;
they go about in darkness;
    all the foundations of the earth are shaken.

Now I say to you, 'You are gods,
    and all of you children of the Most High;

Nevertheless, you shall die like mortals,
    and fall like any prince.'"

Arise, O God, and rule the earth,
    for you shall take all nations for your own.

◯ PSALM 137

You were taken captive by foreign thoughts and noticed yourself being led off. But repenting, you stopped from following through and got a hold of yourself, even while remaining among those sinning. Sit down and weep (as the people did then), saying the words in Psalm 137.

By the waters of Babylon we sat down and wept,
    when we remembered you, O Zion.

As for our harps, we hung them up
  on the trees in the midst of that land.

For those who led us away captive asked us for a song,
and our oppressors called for mirth:
  "Sing us one of the songs of Zion."

How shall we sing the LORD's song
  upon an alien soil?

If I forget you, O Jerusalem,
  let my right hand forget its skill.

Let my tongue cleave to the roof of my mouth
if I do not remember you,
  if I do not set Jerusalem above my highest joy.

Remember the day of Jerusalem, O LORD,
against the people of Edom,
  who said, "Down with it! down with it!
  even to the ground!"

O Daughter of Babylon, doomed to destruction,
  happy the one who pays you back
  for what you have done to us!

Happy shall he be who takes your little ones,
  and dashes them against the rock!

～ PSALM 139

Considering temptations as your testing, if you want to give thanks
after the temptations you have Psalm 139.

LORD, you have searched me out and known me;
  you know my sitting down and my rising up;
  you discern my thoughts from afar.

You trace my journeys and my resting-places
   and are acquainted with all my ways.

Indeed, there is not a word on my lips,
   but you, O LORD, know it altogether.

You press upon me behind and before
   and lay your hand upon me.

Such knowledge is too wonderful for me;
   it is so high that I cannot attain to it.

Where can I go then from your Spirit?
   where can I flee from your presence?

If I climb up to heaven, you are there;
   if I make the grave my bed, you are there also.

If I take the wings of the morning
   and dwell in the uttermost parts of the sea,

Even there your hand will lead me
   and your right hand hold me fast.

If I say, "Surely the darkness will cover me,
   and the light around me turn to night,"

Darkness is not dark to you;
the night is as bright as the day;
   darkness and light to you are both alike.

For you yourself created my inmost parts;
   you knit me together in my mother's womb.

I will thank you because I am marvelously made;
   your works are wonderful, and I know it well.

My body was not hidden from you,
   while I was being made in secret
   and woven in the depths of the earth.

Your eyes beheld my limbs, yet unfinished in the womb;
all of them were written in your book;
    they were fashioned day by day,
    when as yet there was none of them.

How deep I find your thoughts, O God!
    how great is the sum of them!

If I were to count them, they would be more in number
        than the sand;
    to count them all, my life span would need to
        be like yours.

Oh, that you would slay the wicked, O God!
    You that thirst for blood, depart from me.

They speak despitefully against you;
    your enemies take your Name in vain.

Do I not hate those, O LORD, who hate you?
    and do I not loathe those who rise up against you?

I hate them with a perfect hatred;
    they have become my own enemies.

Search me out, O God, and know my heart;
    try me and know my restless thoughts.

Look well whether there be any wickedness in me
    and lead me in the way that is everlasting.

FIVE

Psalms for the Thankful

PSALMS 4, 75, AND 116:1–8*

If after being afflicted you called out to the Lord, and having been heard, you want to give thanks, sing Psalms 4, 75, and 116:1–8.

∾ PSALM 4

Answer me when I call, O God, defender of my cause;
 you set me free when I am hard-pressed;
 have mercy on me and hear my prayer.

"You mortals, how long will you dishonor my glory;
 how long will you worship dumb idols
 and run after false gods?"

Know that the LORD does wonders for the faithful;
 when I call upon the LORD, he will hear me.

Tremble, then, and do not sin;
 speak to your heart in silence upon your bed.

Offer the appointed sacrifices
 and put your trust in the LORD.

Many are saying, "Oh, that we might see better times!"
 Lift up the light of your countenance upon us, O LORD.

You have put gladness in my heart,
 more than when grain and wine and oil increase.

I lie down in peace; at once I fall asleep;
 for only you, LORD, make me dwell in safety.

*Athanasius's LXX version of Psalm 114 corresponds to Psalm 116:1–8 in the BCP.

～ PSALM 75

We give you thanks, O God, we give you thanks,
  calling upon your Name and declaring all your
    wonderful deeds.

"I will appoint a time," says God;
  "I will judge with equity.

Though the earth and all its inhabitants are quaking,
  I will make its pillars fast.

I will say to the boasters, 'Boast no more,'
  and to the wicked, 'Do not toss your horns;

Do not toss your horns so high,
  nor speak with a proud neck.'"

For judgment is neither from the east nor from the west,
  nor yet from the wilderness or the mountains.

 It is God who judges;
  he puts down one and lifts up another.

For in the LORD's hand there is a cup,
full of spiced and foaming wine, which he pours out,
  and all the wicked of the earth shall drink and
    drain the dregs.

But I will rejoice for ever;
  I will sing praises to the God of Jacob.

He shall break off all the horns of the wicked;
  but the horns of the righteous shall be exalted.

∽ PSALM 116:1–8

I love the LORD, because he has heard the voice of
> my supplication,
> because he has inclined his ear to me whenever
> > I called upon him.

The cords of death entangled me;
the grip of the grave took hold of me;
> I came to grief and sorrow.

Then I called upon the Name of the LORD:
> "O LORD, I pray you, save my life."

Gracious is the LORD and righteous;
> our God is full of compassion.

The LORD watches over the innocent;
> I was brought very low, and he helped me.

Turn again to your rest, O my soul,
> for the LORD has treated you well.

For you have rescued my life from death,
> my eyes from tears, and my feet from stumbling.

I will walk in the presence of the LORD
> in the land of the living.

∽ PSALM 8

When you see the grace of the Savior extending everywhere, and the
human race being saved, if you want to salute the Lord, sing Psalm 8.

O LORD our Governor,
> how exalted is your Name in all the world!

Out of the mouths of infants and children
> your majesty is praised above the heavens.

You have set up a stronghold against your adversaries,
to quell the enemy and the avenger.

When I consider your heavens, the work of your fingers,
the moon and the stars you have set in their courses,

What is man that you should be mindful of him?
the son of man that you should seek him out?

You have made him but little lower than the angels;
you adorn him with glory and honor;

You give him mastery over the works of your hands;
you put all things under his feet:

All sheep and oxen,
even the wild beasts of the field,

The birds of the air, the fish of the sea,
and whatsoever walks in the paths of the sea.

O Lord our Governor,
how exalted is your Name in all the world!

PSALMS 9 AND 10

When the Enemy is defeated and the creation saved, do not take credit
yourself, but know that the Son of God accomplished this, and speak
to him in the words of Psalms 9 and 10.*

ᔓ PSALM 9

I will give thanks to you, O Lord, with my whole heart;
I will tell of all your marvelous works.

I will be glad and rejoice in you;
I will sing to your Name, O Most High.

* Athanasius's LXX version of Psalm 9 corresponds to Psalms 9 and 10 of the BCP.

When my enemies are driven back,
     they will stumble and perish at your presence.

For you have maintained my right and my cause;
     you sit upon your throne judging right.

You have rebuked the ungodly and destroyed the wicked;
     you have blotted out their name for ever and ever.

As for the enemy, they are finished, in perpetual ruin,
     their cities ploughed under, the memory of them perished;

But the LORD is enthroned for ever;
     he has set up his throne for judgment.

It is he who rules the world with righteousness;
     he judges the peoples with equity.

The LORD will be a refuge for the oppressed,
     a refuge in time of trouble.

Those who know your Name will put their trust in you,
     for you never forsake those who seek you, O LORD.

Sing praise to the LORD who dwells in Zion;
     proclaim to the peoples the things he has done.

The Avenger of blood will remember them;
     he will not forget the cry of the afflicted.

Have pity on me, O LORD;
     see the misery I suffer from those who hate me,
     O you who lift me up from the gate of death;

So that I may tell of all your praises
and rejoice in your salvation
     in the gates of the city of Zion.

The ungodly have fallen into the pit they dug,
     and in the snare they set is their own foot caught.

The LORD is known by his acts of justice;
    the wicked are trapped in the works of their own hands.

The wicked shall be given over to the grave,
    and also all the peoples that forget God.

For the needy shall not always be forgotten,
    and the hope of the poor shall not perish for ever.

Rise up, O LORD, let not the ungodly have the upper hand;
    let them be judged before you.

Put fear upon them, O LORD;
    let the ungodly know they are but mortal.

⌒ PSALM 10

Why do you stand so far off, O LORD,
    and hide yourself in time of trouble?

The wicked arrogantly persecute the poor,
    but they are trapped in the schemes they have devised.

The wicked boast of their heart's desire;
    the covetous curse and revile the LORD.

The wicked are so proud that they care not for God;
    their only thought is, "God does not matter."

Their ways are devious at all times;
your judgments are far above out of their sight;
    they defy all their enemies.

They say in their heart, "I shall not be shaken;
    no harm shall happen to me ever."

Their mouth is full of cursing, deceit, and oppression;
    under their tongue are mischief and wrong.

They lurk in ambush in public squares
and in secret places they murder the innocent;
>   they spy out the helpless.

They lie in wait, like a lion in a covert;
they lie in wait to seize upon the lowly;
>   they seize the lowly and drag them away in their net.

The innocent are broken and humbled before them;
>   the helpless fall before their power.

They say in their heart, "God has forgotten;
>   he hides his face; he will never notice."

Rise up, O LORD;
lift up your hand, O God;
>   do not forget the afflicted.

Why should the wicked revile God?
>   why should they say in their heart, "You do not care"?

Surely, you behold trouble and misery;
>   you see it and take it into your own hand.

The helpless commit themselves to you,
>   for you are the helper of orphans.

Break the power of the wicked and evil;
>   search out their wickedness until you find none.

The LORD is King for ever and ever;
>   the ungodly shall perish from his land.

The LORD will hear the desire of the humble;
>   you will strengthen their heart and your ears shall hear;

To give justice to the orphan and oppressed,
>   so that mere mortals may strike terror no more.

⌖ PSALM 18

When you have been saved from your enemies and rescued from those pursuing you, sing Psalm 18.

I love you, O LORD my strength,
   O LORD my stronghold, my crag, and my haven.

My God, my rock in whom I put my trust,
   my shield, the horn of my salvation, and my refuge;
   you are worthy of praise.

I will call upon the LORD,
   and so shall I be saved from my enemies.

The breakers of death rolled over me,
   and the torrents of oblivion made me afraid.

The cords of hell entangled me,
   and the snares of death were set for me.

I called upon the LORD in my distress
   and cried out to my God for help.

He heard my voice from his heavenly dwelling;
   my cry of anguish came to his ears.

The earth reeled and rocked;
the roots of the mountains shook;
   they reeled because of his anger.

Smoke rose from his nostrils
and a consuming fire out of his mouth;
   hot burning coals blazed forth from him.

He parted the heavens and came down
   with a storm cloud under his feet.

He mounted on cherubim and flew;
   he swooped on the wings of the wind.

He wrapped darkness about him;
    he made dark waters and thick clouds his pavilion.

From the brightness of his presence, through the clouds,
    burst hailstones and coals of fire.

The LORD thundered out of heaven;
    the Most High uttered his voice.

He loosed his arrows and scattered them;
    he hurled thunderbolts and routed them.

The beds of the seas were uncovered,
and the foundations of the world laid bare,
    at your battle cry, O LORD,
    at the blast of the breath of your nostrils.

He reached down from on high and grasped me;
    he drew me out of great waters.

He delivered me from my strong enemies
and from those who hated me;
    for they were too mighty for me.

They confronted me in the day of my disaster;
    but the LORD was my support.

He brought me out into an open place;
    he rescued me because he delighted in me.

The LORD rewarded me because of my righteous dealing;
    because my hands were clean he rewarded me;

For I have kept the ways of the LORD
    and have not offended against my God;

For all his judgments are before my eyes,
    and his decrees I have not put away from me;

For I have been blameless with him
    and have kept myself from iniquity;

Therefore the LORD rewarded me according to my
        righteous dealing,
    because of the cleanness of my hands in his sight.

With the faithful you show yourself faithful, O God;
    with the forthright you show yourself forthright.

With the pure you show yourself pure,
    but with the crooked you are wily.

You will save a lowly people,
    but you will humble the haughty eyes.

You, O LORD, are my lamp;
    my God, you make my darkness bright.

With you I will break down an enclosure;
    with the help of my God I will scale any wall.

As for God, his ways are perfect;
the words of the LORD are tried in the fire;
    he is a shield to all who trust in him.

For who is God, but the LORD?
    who is the Rock, except our God?

It is God who girds me about with strength
    and makes my way secure.

He makes me sure-footed like a deer
    and lets me stand firm on the heights.

He trains my hands for battle
    and my arms for bending even a bow of bronze.

You have given me your shield of victory;
    your right hand also sustains me;
    your loving care makes me great.

You lengthen my stride beneath me,
    and my ankles do not give way.

I pursue my enemies and overtake them;
    I will not turn back till I have destroyed them.

I strike them down, and they cannot rise;
    they fall defeated at my feet.

You have girded me with strength for the battle;
    you have cast down my adversaries beneath me;
    you have put my enemies to flight.

I destroy those who hate me;
they cry out, but there is none to help them;
    they cry to the LORD, but he does not answer.

I beat them small like dust before the wind;
    I trample them like mud in the streets.

You deliver me from the strife of the peoples;
    you put me at the head of the nations.

A people I have not known shall serve me;
no sooner shall they hear than they shall obey me;
    strangers will cringe before me.

The foreign peoples will lose heart;
    they shall come trembling out of their strongholds.

The LORD lives! Blessed is my Rock!
    Exalted is the God of my salvation!

He is the God who gave me victory
    and cast down the peoples beneath me.

You rescued me from the fury of my enemies;
you exalted me above those who rose against me;
    you saved me from my deadly foe.

Therefore will I extol you among the nations, O LORD,
  and sing praises to your Name.

He multiplies the victories of his king;
  he shows loving-kindness to his anointed,
    to David and his descendants for ever.

∾ PSALM 23

When you realize that you are being shepherded and carefully led by the Lord, be glad in this and sing Psalm 23.

The LORD is my shepherd;
  I shall not be in want.

He makes me lie down in green pastures
  and leads me beside still waters.

He revives my soul
  and guides me along right pathways for his Name's sake.

Though I walk through the valley of the shadow of death,
I shall fear no evil;
  for you are with me;
  your rod and your staff, they comfort me.

You spread a table before me in the presence of those
        who trouble me;
  you have anointed my head with oil,
  and my cup is running over.

Surely your goodness and mercy shall follow me all the days
        of my life,
  and I will dwell in the house of the LORD for ever.

⁓ PSALM 34

If after having fallen among enemies and cleverly escaping them you frustrated their schemes and want to give thanks, then gather together humble people and sing to them Psalm 34.

I will bless the LORD at all times;
    his praise shall ever be in my mouth.

I will glory in the LORD;
    let the humble hear and rejoice.

Proclaim with me the greatness of the LORD;
    let us exalt his Name together.

I sought the LORD, and he answered me
    and delivered me out of all my terror.

Look upon him and be radiant,
    and let not your faces be ashamed.

I called in my affliction and the LORD heard me
    and saved me from all my troubles.

The angel of the LORD encompasses those who fear him,
    and he will deliver them.

Taste and see that the LORD is good;
    happy are they who trust in him!

Fear the LORD, you that are his saints,
    for those who fear him lack nothing.

The young lions lack and suffer hunger,
    but those who seek the LORD lack nothing that is good.

Come, children, and listen to me;
    I will teach you the fear of the LORD.

Who among you loves life
    and desires long life to enjoy prosperity?

Keep your tongue from evil-speaking
 and your lips from lying words.

Turn from evil and do good;
 seek peace and pursue it.

The eyes of the LORD are upon the righteous,
 and his ears are open to their cry.

The face of the LORD is against those who do evil,
 to root out the remembrance of them from the earth.

The righteous cry, and the LORD hears them
 and delivers them from all their troubles.

The LORD is near to the brokenhearted
 and will save those whose spirits are crushed.

Many are the troubles of the righteous,
 but the LORD will deliver him out of them all.

He will keep safe all his bones;
 not one of them shall be broken.

Evil shall slay the wicked,
 and those who hate the righteous will be punished.

The LORD ransoms the life of his servants,
 and none will be punished who trust in him.

⤴ PSALM 46

Having run to God for refuge and having been protected from the trouble happening all around you, if you want to thank God and describe the details of his loving care for you, then you have Psalm 46.

God is our refuge and strength,
 a very present help in trouble.

Therefore we will not fear, though the earth be moved,
    and though the mountains be toppled into the
        depths of the sea;

Though its waters rage and foam,
    and though the mountains tremble at its tumult.

The LORD of hosts is with us;
    the God of Jacob is our stronghold.

There is a river whose streams make glad the city of God,
    the holy habitation of the Most High.

God is in the midst of her;
she shall not be overthrown;
    God shall help her at the break of day.

The nations make much ado, and the kingdoms are shaken;
    God has spoken, and the earth shall melt away.

The LORD of hosts is with us;
    the God of Jacob is our stronghold.

Come now and look upon the works of the LORD,
    what awesome things he has done on earth.

It is he who makes war to cease in all the world;
    he breaks the bow, and shatters the spear,
    and burns the shields with fire.

"Be still, then, and know that I am God;
    I will be exalted among the nations;
    I will be exalted in the earth."

The LORD of hosts is with us;
    the God of Jacob is our stronghold.

⌒ PSALM 65

Whenever you want to praise the Lord, sing the words in Psalm 65.

You are to be praised, O God, in Zion;
> to you shall vows be performed in Jerusalem.

To you that hear prayer shall all flesh come,
> because of their transgressions.

Our sins are stronger than we are,
> but you will blot them out.

Happy are they whom you choose
and draw to your courts to dwell there!
> they will be satisfied by the beauty of your house,
> by the holiness of your temple.

Awesome things will you show us in your righteousness,
O God of our salvation,
> O Hope of all the ends of the earth
> and of the seas that are far away.

You make fast the mountains by your power;
> they are girded about with might.

You still the roaring of the seas,
> the roaring of their waves,
> and the clamor of the peoples.

Those who dwell at the ends of the earth will tremble at your
> marvelous signs;
> you make the dawn and the dusk to sing for joy.

You visit the earth and water it abundantly;
you make it very plenteous;
> the river of God is full of water.

You prepare the grain,
>for so you provide for the earth.
You drench the furrows and smooth out the ridges;
>with heavy rain you soften the ground and bless its increase.

You crown the year with your goodness,
>and your paths overflow with plenty.

May the fields of the wilderness be rich for grazing,
>and the hills be clothed with joy.

May the meadows cover themselves with flocks,
and the valleys cloak themselves with grain;
>let them shout for joy and sing.

PSALMS 85 AND 126

When the anger has come to an end and you are set free from captivity, if you want to give thanks, you may say the words in Psalms 85 and 126.

∽ PSALM 85

You have been gracious to your land, O LORD,
>you have restored the good fortune of Jacob.

You have forgiven the iniquity of your people
>and blotted out all their sins.

You have withdrawn all your fury
>and turned yourself from your wrathful indignation.

Restore us then, O God our Savior;
>let your anger depart from us.

Will you be displeased with us for ever?
>will you prolong your anger from age to age?

Will you not give us life again,
    that your people may rejoice in you?

Show us your mercy, O LORD,
    and grant us your salvation.

I will listen to what the LORD God is saying,
    for he is speaking peace to his faithful people
    and to those who turn their hearts to him.

Truly, his salvation is very near to those who fear him,
    that his glory may dwell in our land.

Mercy and truth have met together;
    righteousness and peace have kissed each other.

Truth shall spring up from the earth,
    and righteousness shall look down from heaven.

The LORD will indeed grant prosperity,
    and our land will yield its increase.

Righteousness shall go before him,
    and peace shall be a pathway for his feet.

～ PSALM 126

When the LORD restored the fortunes of Zion,
    then were we like those who dream.

Then was our mouth filled with laughter,
    and our tongue with shouts of joy.

Then they said among the nations,
    "The LORD has done great things for them."

The LORD has done great things for us,
    and we are glad indeed.

Restore our fortunes, O LORD,
   like the watercourses of the Negev.

Those who sowed with tears
   will reap with songs of joy.

Those who go out weeping, carrying the seed,
   will come again with joy, shouldering their sheaves.

∽ PSALM 98

Do you want to sing to the Lord? You have the words of Psalms 93
and 98.

Sing to the LORD a new song,
   for he has done marvelous things.

With his right hand and his holy arm
   has he won for himself the victory.

The LORD has made known his victory;
   his righteousness has he openly shown in
      the sight of the nations.

He remembers his mercy and faithfulness to
      the house of Israel,
   and all the ends of the earth have seen the
      victory of our God.

Shout with joy to the LORD, all you lands;
   lift up your voice, rejoice, and sing.

Sing to the LORD with the harp,
   with the harp and the voice of song.

With trumpets and the sound of the horn
   shout with joy before the King, the LORD.

Let the sea make a noise and all that is in it,
    the lands and those who dwell therein.

Let the rivers clap their hands,
    and let the hills ring out with joy before the LORD,
    when he comes to judge the earth.

In righteousness shall he judge the world
    and the peoples with equity.

PSALMS 103 AND 104

Since it is fitting for us to thank God through all things and in all things, when you want to bless him, to encourage your soul for this task you have the words of Psalms 103 and 104.

∽ PSALM 103

Bless the LORD, O my soul,
    and all that is within me, bless his holy Name.

Bless the LORD, O my soul,
    and forget not all his benefits.

He forgives all your sins
    and heals all your infirmities;

He redeems your life from the grave
    and crowns you with mercy and loving-kindness;

He satisfies you with good things,
    and your youth is renewed like an eagle's.

The LORD executes righteousness
    and judgment for all who are oppressed.

He made his ways known to Moses
    and his works to the children of Israel.

The LORD is full of compassion and mercy,
    slow to anger and of great kindness.

He will not always accuse us,
    nor will he keep his anger for ever.

He has not dealt with us according to our sins,
    nor rewarded us according to our wickedness.

For as the heavens are high above the earth,
    so is his mercy great upon those who fear him.

As far as the east is from the west,
    so far has he removed our sins from us.

As a father cares for his children,
    so does the LORD care for those who fear him.

For he himself knows whereof we are made;
    he remembers that we are but dust.

Our days are like the grass;
    we flourish like a flower of the field;

When the wind goes over it, it is gone,
    and its place shall know it no more.

But the merciful goodness of the LORD endures for ever
        on those who fear him,
    and his righteousness on children's children;

On those who keep his covenant
    and remember his commandments and do them.

The LORD has set his throne in heaven,
    and his kingship has dominion over all.

Bless the LORD, you angels of his,
you mighty ones who do his bidding,
    and hearken to the voice of his word.

Bless the LORD, all you his hosts,
   you ministers of his who do his will.

Bless the LORD, all you works of his,
in all places of his dominion;
   bless the LORD, O my soul.

∾ PSALM 104

Bless the LORD, O my soul;
   O LORD my God, how excellent is your greatness!
   you are clothed with majesty and splendor.

You wrap yourself with light as with a cloak
   and spread out the heavens like a curtain.

You lay the beams of your chambers in the waters above;
   you make the clouds your chariot;
   you ride on the wings of the wind.

You make the winds your messengers
   and flames of fire your servants.

You have set the earth upon its foundations,
   so that it never shall move at any time.

You covered it with the Deep as with a mantle;
   the waters stood higher than the mountains.

At your rebuke they fled;
   at the voice of your thunder they hastened away.

They went up into the hills and down to the valleys beneath,
   to the places you had appointed for them.

You set the limits that they should not pass;
   they shall not again cover the earth.

You send the springs into the valleys;
    they flow between the mountains.

All the beasts of the field drink their fill from them,
    and the wild asses quench their thirst.

Beside them the birds of the air make their nests
    and sing among the branches.

You water the mountains from your dwelling on high;
    the earth is fully satisfied by the fruit of your works.

You make grass grow for flocks and herds
    and plants to serve mankind;

That they may bring forth food from the earth,
    and wine to gladden our hearts,

Oil to make a cheerful countenance,
    and bread to strengthen the heart.

The trees of the LORD are full of sap,
    the cedars of Lebanon which he planted,

In which the birds build their nests,
    and in whose tops the stork makes his dwelling.

The high hills are a refuge for the mountain goats,
    and the stony cliffs for the rock badgers.

You appointed the moon to mark the seasons,
    and the sun knows the time of its setting.

You make darkness that it may be night,
    in which all the beasts of the forest prowl.

The lions roar after their prey
    and seek their food from God.

The sun rises, and they slip away
    and lay themselves down in their dens.

Man goes forth to his work
    and to his labor until the evening.

O LORD, how manifold are your works!
    in wisdom you have made them all;
    the earth is full of your creatures.

Yonder is the great and wide sea
with its living things too many to number,
    creatures both small and great.

There move the ships,
and there is that Leviathan,
    which you have made for the sport of it.

All of them look to you
    to give them their food in due season.

You give it to them; they gather it;
    you open your hand, and they are filled with good things.

You hide your face, and they are terrified;
    you take away their breath,
    and they die and return to their dust.

You send forth your Spirit, and they are created;
    and so you renew the face of the earth.

May the glory of the LORD endure for ever;
    may the LORD rejoice in all his works.

He looks at the earth and it trembles;
    he touches the mountains and they smoke.

I will sing to the LORD as long as I live;
    I will praise my God while I have my being.

May these words of mine please him;
    I will rejoice in the LORD.

Let sinners be consumed out of the earth,
and the wicked be no more.

Bless the LORD, O my soul.
Hallelujah!

PSALMS 105, 111, 118, AND 138

When you feel the need to give thanks, sing Psalms 9, 75, 92, 105,
106, 107, 108, 111, 118, 136, and 138.

∽ PSALM 105

Give thanks to the LORD and call upon his Name;
make known his deeds among the peoples.

Sing to him, sing praises to him,
and speak of all his marvelous works.

Glory in his holy Name;
let the hearts of those who seek the LORD rejoice.

Search for the LORD and his strength;
continually seek his face.

Remember the marvels he has done,
his wonders and the judgments of his mouth,

O offspring of Abraham his servant,
O children of Jacob his chosen.

He is the LORD our God;
his judgments prevail in all the world.

He has always been mindful of his covenant,
the promise he made for a thousand generations:

The covenant he made with Abraham,
the oath that he swore to Isaac,

Which he established as a statute for Jacob,
an everlasting covenant for Israel,

Saying, "To you will I give the land of Canaan
to be your allotted inheritance."

When they were few in number,
of little account, and sojourners in the land,

Wandering from nation to nation
and from one kingdom to another,

He let no one oppress them
and rebuked kings for their sake,

Saying, "Do not touch my anointed
and do my prophets no harm."

Then he called for a famine in the land
and destroyed the supply of bread.

He sent a man before them,
Joseph, who was sold as a slave.

They bruised his feet in fetters;
his neck they put in an iron collar.

Until his prediction came to pass,
the word of the LORD tested him.

The king sent and released him;
the ruler of the peoples set him free.

He set him as a master over his household,
as a ruler over all his possessions,

To instruct his princes according to his will
and to teach his elders wisdom.

Israel came into Egypt,
and Jacob became a sojourner in the land of Ham.

The LORD made his people exceedingly fruitful;
    he made them stronger than their enemies;

Whose heart he turned, so that they hated his people,
    and dealt unjustly with his servants.

He sent Moses his servant,
    and Aaron whom he had chosen.

They worked his signs among them,
    and portents in the land of Ham.

He sent darkness, and it grew dark;
    but the Egyptians rebelled against his words.

He turned their waters into blood
    and caused their fish to die.

Their land was overrun by frogs,
    in the very chambers of their kings.

He spoke, and there came swarms of insects
    and gnats within all their borders.

He gave them hailstones instead of rain,
    and flames of fire throughout their land.

He blasted their vines and their fig trees
    and shattered every tree in their country.

He spoke, and the locust came,
    and young locusts without number,

Which ate up all the green plants in their land
    and devoured the fruit of their soil.

He struck down the firstborn of their land,
    the firstfruits of all their strength.

He led out his people with silver and gold;
    in all their tribes there was not one that stumbled.

Egypt was glad of their going,
    because they were afraid of them.

He spread out a cloud for a covering
    and a fire to give light in the night season.

They asked, and quails appeared,
    and he satisfied them with bread from heaven.

He opened the rock, and water flowed,
    so the river ran in the dry places.

For God remembered his holy word
    and Abraham his servant.

So he led forth his people with gladness,
    his chosen with shouts of joy.

He gave his people the lands of the nations,
    and they took the fruit of others' toil,

That they might keep his statutes
    and observe his laws.
    Hallelujah!

∽ PSALM 111

Hallelujah!
I will give thanks to the LORD with my whole heart,
    in the assembly of the upright, in the congregation.

Great are the deeds of the LORD!
    they are studied by all who delight in them.

His work is full of majesty and splendor,
    and his righteousness endures for ever.

He makes his marvelous works to be remembered;
    the LORD is gracious and full of compassion.

He gives food to those who fear him;
    he is ever mindful of his covenant.

He has shown his people the power of his works
    in giving them the lands of the nations.

The works of his hands are faithfulness and justice;
    all his commandments are sure.

They stand fast for ever and ever,
    because they are done in truth and equity.

He sent redemption to his people;
he commanded his covenant for ever;
    holy and awesome is his Name.

The fear of the LORD is the beginning of wisdom;
    those who act accordingly have a good understanding;
    his praise endures for ever.

PSALM 118

Give thanks to the LORD, for he is good;
    his mercy endures for ever.

Let Israel now proclaim,
    "His mercy endures for ever."

Let the house of Aaron now proclaim,
    "His mercy endures for ever."

Let those who fear the LORD now proclaim,
    "His mercy endures for ever."

I called to the LORD in my distress;
    the LORD answered by setting me free.

The LORD is at my side, therefore I will not fear;
    what can anyone do to me?

The LORD is at my side to help me;
 I will triumph over those who hate me.

It is better to rely on the LORD
 than to put any trust in flesh.

It is better to rely on the LORD
 than to put any trust in rulers.

All the ungodly encompass me;
 in the name of the LORD I will repel them.

They hem me in, they hem me in on every side;
 in the name of the LORD I will repel them.

They swarm about me like bees;
they blaze like a fire of thorns;
 in the name of the LORD I will repel them.

I was pressed so hard that I almost fell,
 but the LORD came to my help.

The LORD is my strength and my song,
 and he has become my salvation.

There is a sound of exultation and victory
 in the tents of the righteous:

"The right hand of the LORD has triumphed!
 the right hand of the LORD is exalted!
 the right hand of the LORD has triumphed!"

I shall not die, but live,
 and declare the works of the LORD.

The LORD has punished me sorely,
 but he did not hand me over to death.

Open for me the gates of righteousness;
    I will enter them;
    I will offer thanks to the LORD.

"This is the gate of the LORD;
    he who is righteous may enter."

I will give thanks to you, for you answered me
    and have become my salvation.

The same stone which the builders rejected
    has become the chief cornerstone.

This is the LORD'S doing,
    and it is marvelous in our eyes.

On this day the LORD has acted;
    we will rejoice and be glad in it.

Hosannah, LORD, hosannah!
    LORD, send us now success.

Blessed is he who comes in the name of the Lord;
    we bless you from the house of the LORD.
God is the LORD; he has shined upon us;
    form a procession with branches up to the horns of the altar.

"You are my God, and I will thank you;
    you are my God, and I will exalt you."

Give thanks to the LORD, for he is good;
    his mercy endures for ever.

⌒ PSALM 138

I will give thanks to you, O LORD, with my whole heart;
  before the gods I will sing your praise.

I will bow down toward your holy temple
and praise your Name,
  because of your love and faithfulness;

For you have glorified your Name
  and your word above all things.

When I called, you answered me;
  you increased my strength within me.

All the kings of the earth will praise you, O LORD,
  when they have heard the words of your mouth.

They will sing of the ways of the LORD,
  that great is the glory of the LORD.

Though the LORD be high, he cares for the lowly;
  he perceives the haughty from afar.

Though I walk in the midst of trouble, you keep me safe;
  you stretch forth your hand against the fury of my enemies;
  your right hand shall save me.

The LORD will make good his purpose for me;
  O LORD, your love endures for ever;
  do not abandon the works of your hands.

PSALMS 106, 113, 117, 136, 146, AND 149

If you want to sing Psalms full of "Hallelujah," you have Psalms 105, 106, 107, 112, 113, 114, 115, 116, 117, 118, 119, 135, 136, 146, 147, 148, 149, and 150.

∼ PSALM 106

Hallelujah!
Give thanks to the LORD, for he is good,
   for his mercy endures for ever.

Who can declare the mighty acts of the LORD
   or show forth all his praise?

Happy are those who act with justice
   and always do what is right!

Remember me, O LORD, with the favor you have
               for your people,
   and visit me with your saving help;

That I may see the prosperity of your elect
and be glad with the gladness of your people,
   that I may glory with your inheritance.

We have sinned as our forebears did;
   we have done wrong and dealt wickedly.

In Egypt they did not consider your marvelous works,
nor remember the abundance of your love;
   they defied the Most High at the Red Sea.

But he saved them for his Name's sake,
   to make his power known.

He rebuked the Red Sea, and it dried up,
   and he led them through the deep as through a desert.

He saved them from the hand of those who hated them
    and redeemed them from the hand of the enemy.

The waters covered their oppressors;
    not one of them was left.

Then they believed his words
    and sang him songs of praise.

But they soon forgot his deeds
    and did not wait for his counsel.

A craving seized them in the wilderness,
    and they put God to the test in the desert.

He gave them what they asked,
    but sent leanness into their soul.

They envied Moses in the camp,
    and Aaron, the holy one of the LORD.

The earth opened and swallowed Dathan
    and covered the company of Abiram.

Fire blazed up against their company,
    and flames devoured the wicked.

Israel made a bull-calf at Horeb
    and worshiped a molten image;

And so they exchanged their Glory
    for the image of an ox that feeds on grass.

They forgot God their Savior,
    who had done great things in Egypt,

Wonderful deeds in the land of Ham,
    and fearful things at the Red Sea.

So he would have destroyed them,
had not Moses his chosen stood before him in the breach,
    to turn away his wrath from consuming them.

They refused the pleasant land
  and would not believe his promise.

They grumbled in their tents
  and would not listen to the voice of the LORD.

So he lifted his hand against them,
  to overthrow them in the wilderness,

To cast out their seed among the nations,
  and to scatter them throughout the lands.

They joined themselves to Baal-Peor
  and ate sacrifices offered to the dead.

They provoked him to anger with their actions,
  and a plague broke out among them.

Then Phinehas stood up and interceded,
  and the plague came to an end.

This was reckoned to him as righteousness
  throughout all generations for ever.

Again they provoked his anger at the waters of Meribah,
  so that he punished Moses because of them;

For they so embittered his spirit
  that he spoke rash words with his lips.

They did not destroy the peoples
  as the LORD had commanded them.

They intermingled with the heathen
  and learned their pagan ways,

So that they worshiped their idols,
  which became a snare to them.

They sacrificed their sons
  and their daughters to evil spirits.

They shed innocent blood,
the blood of their sons and daughters,
    which they offered to the idols of Canaan,
    and the land was defiled with blood.

Thus they were polluted by their actions
    and went whoring in their evil deeds.

Therefore the wrath of the LORD was kindled against
            his people
    and he abhorred his inheritance.

He gave them over to the hand of the heathen,
    and those who hated them ruled over them.

Their enemies oppressed them,
    and they were humbled under their hand.

Many a time did he deliver them,
but they rebelled through their own devices,
    and were brought down in their iniquity.

Nevertheless, he saw their distress,
    when he heard their lamentation.

He remembered his covenant with them
    and relented in accordance with his great mercy.

He caused them to be pitied
    by those who held them captive.

Save us, O LORD our God,
and gather us from among the nations,
    that we may give thanks to your holy Name
    and glory in your praise.

Blessed be the LORD, the God of Israel,
from everlasting and to everlasting;
    and let all the people say, "Amen!"
    Hallelujah!

∽ PSALM 113

Hallelujah!
Give praise, you servants of the LORD;
    praise the Name of the LORD.

Let the Name of the LORD be blessed,
    from this time forth for evermore.

From the rising of the sun to its going down
    let the Name of the LORD be praised.

The LORD is high above all nations,
    and his glory above the heavens.

Who is like the LORD our God, who sits enthroned on high,
    but stoops to behold the heavens and the earth?

He takes up the weak out of the dust
    and lifts up the poor from the ashes.

He sets them with the princes,
    with the princes of his people.

He makes the woman of a childless house
    to be a joyful mother of children.

∽ PSALM 117

Praise the LORD, all you nations;
    laud him, all you peoples.

For his loving-kindness toward us is great,
    and the faithfulness of the LORD endures for ever.
    Hallelujah!

Ꮿ PSALM 136

Give thanks to the LORD, for he is good,
    for his mercy endures for ever.

Give thanks to the God of gods,
    for his mercy endures for ever.

Give thanks to the Lord of lords,
    for his mercy endures for ever.

Who only does great wonders,
    for his mercy endures for ever;

Who by wisdom made the heavens,
    for his mercy endures for ever;

Who spread out the earth upon the waters,
    for his mercy endures for ever;

Who created great lights,
    for his mercy endures for ever;

The sun to rule the day,
    for his mercy endures for ever;

The moon and the stars to govern the night,
    for his mercy endures for ever.

Who struck down the firstborn of Egypt,
    for his mercy endures for ever;

And brought out Israel from among them,
    for his mercy endures for ever;

With a mighty hand and a stretched-out arm,
    for his mercy endures for ever;

Who divided the Red Sea in two,
    for his mercy endures for ever;

And made Israel to pass through the midst of it,
    for his mercy endures for ever;

But swept Pharaoh and his army into the Red Sea,
    for his mercy endures for ever;

Who led his people through the wilderness,
    for his mercy endures for ever.

Who struck down great kings,
    for his mercy endures for ever;

And slew mighty kings,
    for his mercy endures for ever;

Sihon, king of the Amorites,
    for his mercy endures for ever;

And Og, the king of Bashan,
    for his mercy endures for ever;

And gave away their lands for an inheritance,
    for his mercy endures for ever;

An inheritance for Israel his servant,
    for his mercy endures for ever.

Who remembered us in our low estate,
    for his mercy endures for ever;

And delivered us from our enemies,
    for his mercy endures for ever;

Who gives food to all creatures,
    for his mercy endures for ever.

Give thanks to the God of heaven,
    for his mercy endures for ever.

∽ PSALM 146

Hallelujah!
Praise the LORD, O my soul!
    I will praise the LORD as long as I live;
    I will sing praises to my God while I have my being.

Put not your trust in rulers, nor in any child of earth,
    for there is no help in them.

When they breathe their last, they return to earth,
    and in that day their thoughts perish.

Happy are they who have the God of Jacob for their help!
    whose hope is in the LORD their God;

Who made heaven and earth, the seas, and all that is in them;
    who keeps his promise for ever;

Who gives justice to those who are oppressed,
    and food to those who hunger.

The LORD sets the prisoners free;
the LORD opens the eyes of the blind;
    the LORD lifts up those who are bowed down;

The LORD loves the righteous;
the LORD cares for the stranger;
    he sustains the orphan and widow,
    but frustrates the way of the wicked.

The LORD shall reign for ever,
    your God, O Zion, throughout all generations.
    Hallelujah!

∾ PSALM 149

Hallelujah!
Sing to the LORD a new song;
    sing his praise in the congregation of the faithful.

Let Israel rejoice in his Maker;
    let the children of Zion be joyful in their King.

Let them praise his Name in the dance;
    let them sing praise to him with timbrel and harp.

For the LORD takes pleasure in his people
    and adorns the poor with victory.

Let the faithful rejoice in triumph;
    let them be joyful on their beds.

Let the praises of God be in their throat
    and a two-edged sword in their hand;

To wreak vengeance on the nations
    and punishment on the peoples;

To bind their kings in chains
    and their nobles with links of iron;

To inflict on them the judgment decreed;
    this is glory for all his faithful people.
    Hallelujah!

∾ PSALM 145

After marveling at all the wonderful deeds of God and remembering his
goodness to you and to everyone, if you want to bless God for these
things, say the words of David himself, which he said in Psalm 145.

I will exalt you, O God my King,
    and bless your Name for ever and ever.

Every day will I bless you
    and praise your Name for ever and ever.

Great is the LORD and greatly to be praised;
    there is no end to his greatness.

One generation shall praise your works to another
    and shall declare your power.

I will ponder the glorious splendor of your majesty
    and all your marvelous works.

They shall speak of the might of your wondrous acts,
    and I will tell of your greatness.

They shall publish the remembrance of your great goodness;
    they shall sing of your righteous deeds.

The LORD is gracious and full of compassion,
    slow to anger and of great kindness.

The LORD is loving to everyone
    and his compassion is over all his works.

All your works praise you, O LORD,
    and your faithful servants bless you.

They make known the glory of your kingdom
    and speak of your power;

That the peoples may know of your power
    and the glorious splendor of your kingdom.

Your kingdom is an everlasting kingdom;
    your dominion endures throughout all ages.

The LORD is faithful in all his words
    and merciful in all his deeds.

The LORD upholds all those who fall;
    he lifts up those who are bowed down.

The eyes of all wait upon you, O LORD,
    and you give them their food in due season.

You open wide your hand
    and satisfy the needs of every living creature.

The LORD is righteous in all his ways
    and loving in all his works.

The LORD is near to those who call upon him,
    to all who call upon him faithfully.

He fulfills the desire of those who fear him;
    he hears their cry and helps them.

The LORD preserves all those who love him,
    but he destroys all the wicked.

My mouth shall speak the praise of the LORD;
    let all flesh bless his holy Name for ever and ever.

⌐ PSALM 151*

If, being small, you were picked for some position of authority before
your brothers, do not act superior to them, but give glory to the Lord
who chose you and sing Psalm 151, which is David's own.

I was small among my brothers
    and the youngest in the house of my father;
    I would shepherd the sheep of my father.

My hands made an instrument;
    my fingers tuned a harp.

And who will report to my lord?
    The LORD himself, it is he who listens.

* There are 151 psalms in the Septuagint. The translation of this final psalm is from *A New
English Translation of the Septuagint* (NETS), 619–20. Note: I have substituted the NRSV's "Philistine" for NETS's "allophyle."

It was he who sent his messenger
    and took me from the sheep of my father
    and anointed me with the oil of his anointing.

My brothers were handsome and tall,
    and the LORD did not take delight in them.

I went out to meet the Philistine,
    and he cursed me by his idols.

But I, having drawn the dagger from him,
    I beheaded him
    and removed reproach from Israel's sons.

SIX

Psalms for Reflection

⌀ PSALM 2

If you want to condemn the evil plot of the Jews against the Savior, you have Psalm 2.

Why are the nations in an uproar?
    Why do the peoples mutter empty threats?

Why do the kings of the earth rise up in revolt,
and the princes plot together,
    against the LORD and against his Anointed?

"Let us break their yoke," they say;
    "let us cast off their bonds from us."

He whose throne is in heaven is laughing;
    the Lord has them in derision.

Then he speaks to them in his wrath,
    and his rage fills them with terror.

"I myself have set my king
    upon my holy hill of Zion."

Let me announce the decree of the LORD:
    he said to me, "You are my Son;
    this day have I begotten you.

Ask of me, and I will give you the nations for
        your inheritance
and the ends of the earth for your possession.

You shall crush them with an iron rod
  and shatter them like a piece of pottery."

And now, you kings, be wise;
  be warned, you rulers of the earth.

Submit to the LORD with fear,
  and with trembling bow before him;

Lest he be angry and you perish;
  for his wrath is quickly kindled.

Happy are they all
  who take refuge in him!

∽ PSALM 16

Psalm 16 makes known the Savior's resurrection from the dead.

Protect me, O God, for I take refuge in you;
  I have said to the LORD, "You are my Lord,
  my good above all other."

All my delight is upon the godly that are in the land,
  upon those who are noble among the people.

But those who run after other gods
  shall have their troubles multiplied.

Their libations of blood I will not offer,
  nor take the names of their gods upon my lips.

O LORD, you are my portion and my cup;
  it is you who uphold my lot.

My boundaries enclose a pleasant land;
  indeed, I have a goodly heritage.

I will bless the LORD who gives me counsel;
>   my heart teaches me, night after night.

I have set the LORD always before me;
>   because he is at my right hand I shall not fall.

My heart, therefore, is glad, and my spirit rejoices;
>   my body also shall rest in hope.

For you will not abandon me to the grave,
>   nor let your holy one see the Pit.

You will show me the path of life;
>   in your presence there is fullness of joy,
>   and in your right hand are pleasures for evermore.

⌐ PSALM 19

When you marvel at the order of creation, the grace of Providence upon it, and the holy instructions of the law, sing Psalms 19 and 24.

The heavens declare the glory of God,
>   and the firmament shows his handiwork.

One day tells its tale to another,
>   and one night imparts knowledge to another.

Although they have no words or language,
>   and their voices are not heard,

Their sound has gone out into all lands,
>   and their message to the ends of the world.

In the deep has he set a pavilion for the sun;
>   it comes forth like a bridegroom out of his chamber;
>   it rejoices like a champion to run its course.

It goes forth from the uttermost edge of the heavens
and runs about to the end of it again;
    nothing is hidden from its burning heat.

The law of the LORD is perfect
        and revives the soul;
    the testimony of the LORD is sure
        and gives wisdom to the innocent.

The statutes of the LORD are just
        and rejoice the heart;
    the commandment of the LORD is clear
        and gives light to the eyes.

The fear of the LORD is clean
        and endures for ever;
    the judgments of the LORD are true
        and righteous altogether.

More to be desired are they than gold,
        more than much fine gold,
    sweeter far than honey,
        than honey in the comb.

By them also is your servant enlightened,
    and in keeping them there is great reward.

Who can tell how often he offends?
    cleanse me from my secret faults.

Above all, keep your servant from presumptuous sins;
let them not get dominion over me;
    then shall I be whole and sound,
    and innocent of a great offense.

Let the words of my mouth and the meditation of my
        heart be acceptable in your sight,
    O LORD, my strength and my redeemer.

PSALMS 21 AND 72

Psalms 21, 50, and 72 make known the Savior's kingship and just rule, and in turn, his coming in the flesh to us and the calling of the Gentiles.

∽ PSALM 21

The king rejoices in your strength, O LORD;
    how greatly he exults in your victory!

You have given him his heart's desire;
    you have not denied him the request of his lips.

For you meet him with blessings of prosperity,
    and set a crown of fine gold upon his head.

He asked you for life, and you gave it to him:
    length of days, for ever and ever.

His honor is great, because of your victory;
    splendor and majesty have you bestowed upon him.

For you will give him everlasting felicity
    and will make him glad with the joy of your presence.

For the king puts his trust in the LORD;
    because of the loving-kindness of the Most High, he
        will not fall.

Your hand will lay hold upon all your enemies;
    your right hand will seize all those who hate you.

You will make them like a fiery furnace
    at the time of your appearing, O LORD;

You will swallow them up in your wrath,
    and fire shall consume them.

You will destroy their offspring from the land
    and their descendants from among the peoples of the earth.

Though they intend evil against you
and devise wicked schemes,
>> yet they shall not prevail.

For you will put them to flight
>> and aim your arrows at them.

Be exalted, O LORD, in your might;
>> we will sing and praise your power.

⌢ PSALM 72

Give the King your justice, O God,
>> and your righteousness to the King's Son;

That he may rule your people righteously
>> and the poor with justice;

That the mountains may bring prosperity to the people,
>> and the little hills bring righteousness.

He shall defend the needy among the people;
>> he shall rescue the poor and crush the oppressor.

He shall live as long as the sun and moon endure,
>> from one generation to another.

He shall come down like rain upon the mown field,
>> like showers that water the earth.

In his time shall the righteous flourish;
>> there shall be abundance of peace till the moon shall
>>> be no more.

He shall rule from sea to sea,
>> and from the River to the ends of the earth.

His foes shall bow down before him,
>> and his enemies lick the dust.

The kings of Tarshish and of the isles shall pay tribute,
  and the kings of Arabia and Saba offer gifts.

All kings shall bow down before him,
  and all the nations do him service.

For he shall deliver the poor who cries out in distress,
  and the oppressed who has no helper.

He shall have pity on the lowly and poor;
  he shall preserve the lives of the needy.

He shall redeem their lives from oppression and violence,
  and dear shall their blood be in his sight.

Long may he live!
and may there be given to him gold from Arabia;
  may prayer be made for him always,
  and may they bless him all the day long.

May there be abundance of grain on the earth,
growing thick even on the hilltops;
  may its fruit flourish like Lebanon,
  and its grain like grass upon the earth.

May his Name remain for ever
and be established as long as the sun endures;
  may all the nations bless themselves in him and
    call him blessed.

Blessed be the Lord GOD, the God of Israel,
  who alone does wondrous deeds!

And blessed be his glorious Name for ever!
  and may all the earth be filled with his glory.
    Amen. Amen.

⟲ PSALM 32

When you see people being baptized and rescued from a damaged world, and you marvel at God's loving care for human beings, sing for them Psalm 32.

Happy are they whose transgressions are forgiven,
    and whose sin is put away!

Happy are they to whom the LORD imputes no guilt,
    and in whose spirit there is no guile!

While I held my tongue, my bones withered away,
    because of my groaning all day long.

For your hand was heavy upon me day and night;
    my moisture was dried up as in the heat of summer.

Then I acknowledged my sin to you,
    and did not conceal my guilt.

I said, "I will confess my transgressions to the LORD."
    Then you forgave me the guilt of my sin.

Therefore all the faithful will make their prayers to you in
            time of trouble;
    when the great waters overflow, they shall not reach them.

You are my hiding-place;
you preserve me from trouble;
    you surround me with shouts of deliverance.

"I will instruct you and teach you in the way that you
            should go;
    I will guide you with my eye.

Do not be like horse or mule, which have no understanding;
    who must be fitted with bit and bridle,
        or else they will not stay near you."

Great are the tribulations of the wicked;
   but mercy embraces those who trust in the LORD.

Be glad, you righteous, and rejoice in the LORD;
   shout for joy, all who are true of heart.

PSALMS 44, 78, 89, 114, AND 115*

If you want to recount continually the wonderful deeds which God
performed for the patriarchs, such as the Exodus out of Egypt or the
guidance through the wilderness, because God is good but people are
ungrateful, you have Psalms 44, 78, 89, 105, 106, 107, 114, and 115.

⌐ PSALM 44

We have heard with our ears, O God,
our forefathers have told us,
   the deeds you did in their days,
   in the days of old.

How with your hand you drove the peoples out
and planted our forefathers in the land;
   how you destroyed nations and made your people flourish.

For they did not take the land by their sword,
nor did their arm win the victory for them;
   but your right hand, your arm, and the
         light of your countenance,
   because you favored them.

You are my King and my God;
   you command victories for Jacob.

Through you we pushed back our adversaries;
   through your Name we trampled on those who
         rose up against us.

*Athanasius's LXX version of Psalm 113 corresponds to Psalms 114 and 115 of the BCP.

For I do not rely on my bow,
    and my sword does not give me the victory.

Surely, you gave us victory over our adversaries
    and put those who hate us to shame.

Every day we gloried in God,
    and we will praise your Name for ever.

Nevertheless, you have rejected and humbled us
    and do not go forth with our armies.

You have made us fall back before our adversary,
    and our enemies have plundered us.

You have made us like sheep to be eaten
    and have scattered us among the nations.

You are selling your people for a trifle
    and are making no profit on the sale of them.

You have made us the scorn of our neighbors,
    a mockery and derision to those around us.

You have made us a byword among the nations,
    a laughing-stock among the peoples.

My humiliation is daily before me,
    and shame has covered my face;

Because of the taunts of the mockers and blasphemers,
    because of the enemy and avenger.

All this has come upon us;
    yet we have not forgotten you,
    nor have we betrayed your covenant.

Our heart never turned back,
    nor did our footsteps stray from your path;

Though you thrust us down into a place of misery,
    and covered us over with deep darkness.

If we have forgotten the Name of our God,
    or stretched out our hands to some strange god,

Will not God find it out?
    for he knows the secrets of the heart.

Indeed, for your sake we are killed all the day long;
    we are accounted as sheep for the slaughter.

Awake, O Lord! why are you sleeping?
    Arise! do not reject us for ever.

Why have you hidden your face
    and forgotten our affliction and oppression?

We sink down into the dust;
    our body cleaves to the ground.

Rise up, and help us,
    and save us, for the sake of your steadfast love.

⌁ PSALM 78

Hear my teaching, O my people;
    incline your ears to the words of my mouth.

I will open my mouth in a parable;
    I will declare the mysteries of ancient times.

That which we have heard and known,
and what our forefathers have told us,
    we will not hide from their children.

We will recount to generations to come
the praiseworthy deeds and the power of the LORD,
    and the wonderful works he has done.

He gave his decrees to Jacob
and established a law for Israel,
> which he commanded them to teach their children;

That the generations to come might know,
and the children yet unborn;
> that they in their turn might tell it to their children;

So that they might put their trust in God,
> and not forget the deeds of God,
> but keep his commandments;

And not be like their forefathers,
a stubborn and rebellious generation,
> a generation whose heart was not steadfast,
> and whose spirit was not faithful to God.

The people of Ephraim, armed with the bow,
> turned back in the day of battle;

They did not keep the covenant of God,
> and refused to walk in his law;

They forgot what he had done,
> and the wonders he had shown them.

He worked marvels in the sight of their forefathers,
> in the land of Egypt, in the field of Zoan.

He split open the sea and let them pass through;
> he made the waters stand up like walls.

He led them with a cloud by day,
> and all the night through with a glow of fire.

He split the hard rocks in the wilderness
> and gave them drink as from the great deep.

He brought streams out of the cliff,
> and the waters gushed out like rivers.

But they went on sinning against him,
    rebelling in the desert against the Most High.

They tested God in their hearts,
    demanding food for their craving.

They railed against God and said,
    "Can God set a table in the wilderness?

True, he struck the rock, the waters gushed out, and the
                gullies overflowed;
    but is he able to give bread
    or to provide meat for his people?"

When the LORD heard this, he was full of wrath;
    a fire was kindled against Jacob,
    and his anger mounted against Israel;

For they had no faith in God,
    nor did they put their trust in his saving power.

So he commanded the clouds above
    and opened the doors of heaven.

He rained down manna upon them to eat
    and gave them grain from heaven.

So mortals ate the bread of angels;
    he provided for them food enough.

He caused the east wind to blow in the heavens
    and led out the south wind by his might.

He rained down flesh upon them like dust
    and wingèd birds like the sand of the sea.

He let it fall in the midst of their camp
    and round about their dwellings.

So they ate and were well filled,
    for he gave them what they craved.

But they did not stop their craving,
　　though the food was still in their mouths.

So God's anger mounted against them;
　　he slew their strongest men
　　and laid low the youth of Israel.

In spite of all this, they went on sinning
　　and had no faith in his wonderful works.

So he brought their days to an end like a breath
　　and their years in sudden terror.

Whenever he slew them, they would seek him,
　　and repent, and diligently search for God.

They would remember that God was their rock,
　　and the Most High God their redeemer.

But they flattered him with their mouths
　　and lied to him with their tongues.

Their heart was not steadfast toward him,
　　and they were not faithful to his covenant.

But he was so merciful that he forgave their sins
and did not destroy them;
　　many times he held back his anger
　　and did not permit his wrath to be roused.

For he remembered that they were but flesh,
　　a breath that goes forth and does not return.

How often the people disobeyed him in the wilderness
　　and offended him in the desert!

Again and again they tempted God
　　and provoked the Holy One of Israel.

They did not remember his power
    in the day when he ransomed them from the enemy;

How he wrought his signs in Egypt
    and his omens in the field of Zoan.

He turned their rivers into blood,
    so that they could not drink of their streams.

He sent swarms of flies among them, which ate them up,
    and frogs, which destroyed them.

He gave their crops to the caterpillar,
    the fruit of their toil to the locust.

He killed their vines with hail
    and their sycamores with frost.

He delivered their cattle to hailstones
    and their livestock to hot thunderbolts.

He poured out upon them his blazing anger:
    fury, indignation, and distress,
    a troop of destroying angels.

He gave full rein to his anger;
he did not spare their souls from death;
    but delivered their lives to the plague.

He struck down all the firstborn of Egypt,
    the flower of manhood in the dwellings of Ham.

He led out his people like sheep
    and guided them in the wilderness like a flock.

He led them to safety, and they were not afraid;
    but the sea overwhelmed their enemies.

He brought them to his holy land,
    the mountain his right hand had won.

He drove out the Canaanites before them
and apportioned an inheritance to them by lot;
 he made the tribes of Israel to dwell in their tents.

But they tested the Most High God, and defied him,
 and did not keep his commandments.

They turned away and were disloyal like their fathers;
 they were undependable like a warped bow.

They grieved him with their hill-altars
 and provoked his displeasure with their idols.

When God heard this, he was angry
 and utterly rejected Israel.

He forsook the shrine at Shiloh,
 the tabernacle where he had lived among his people.

He delivered the ark into captivity,
 his glory into the adversary's hand.

He gave his people to the sword
 and was angered against his inheritance.

The fire consumed their young men;
 there were no wedding songs for their maidens.

Their priests fell by the sword,
 and their widows made no lamentation.

Then the LORD woke as though from sleep,
 like a warrior refreshed with wine.

He struck his enemies on the backside
 and put them to perpetual shame.

He rejected the tent of Joseph
 and did not choose the tribe of Ephraim;

He chose instead the tribe of Judah
  and Mount Zion, which he loved.

He built his sanctuary like the heights of heaven,
  like the earth which he founded for ever.

He chose David his servant,
  and took him away from the sheepfolds.

He brought him from following the ewes,
  to be a shepherd over Jacob his people
  and over Israel his inheritance.

So he shepherded them with a faithful and true heart
  and guided them with the skillfulness of his hands.

∽ PSALM 89

Your love, O LORD, for ever will I sing;
  from age to age my mouth will proclaim your faithfulness.

For I am persuaded that your love is established for ever;
  you have set your faithfulness firmly in the heavens.

"I have made a covenant with my chosen one;
  I have sworn an oath to David my servant:

'I will establish your line for ever,
  and preserve your throne for all generations.'"

The heavens bear witness to your wonders, O LORD,
  and to your faithfulness in the assembly of the holy ones;

For who in the skies can be compared to the LORD?
  who is like the LORD among the gods?

God is much to be feared in the council of the holy ones,
  great and terrible to all those round about him.

Who is like you, LORD God of hosts?
O mighty LORD, your faithfulness is all around you.

You rule the raging of the sea
and still the surging of its waves.

You have crushed Rahab of the deep with a deadly wound;
you have scattered your enemies with your mighty arm.

Yours are the heavens; the earth also is yours;
you laid the foundations of the world and all that is in it.

You have made the north and the south;
Tabor and Hermon rejoice in your Name.

You have a mighty arm;
strong is your hand and high is your right hand.

Righteousness and justice are the foundations of your throne;
love and truth go before your face.

Happy are the people who know the festal shout!
they walk, O LORD, in the light of your presence.

They rejoice daily in your Name;
they are jubilant in your righteousness.

For you are the glory of their strength,
and by your favor our might is exalted.

Truly, the LORD is our ruler;
the Holy One of Israel is our King.

You spoke once in a vision and said to your faithful people:
"I have set the crown upon a warrior
and have exalted one chosen out of the people.

I have found David my servant;
with my holy oil have I anointed him.

My hand will hold him fast
    and my arm will make him strong.

No enemy shall deceive him,
    nor any wicked man bring him down.

I will crush his foes before him
    and strike down those who hate him.

My faithfulness and love shall be with him,
    and he shall be victorious through my Name.

I shall make his dominion extend
    from the Great Sea to the River.

He will say to me, 'You are my Father,
    my God, and the rock of my salvation.'

I will make him my firstborn
    and higher than the kings of the earth.

I will keep my love for him for ever,
    and my covenant will stand firm for him.

I will establish his line for ever
    and his throne as the days of heaven."

"If his children forsake my law
    and do not walk according to my judgments;

If they break my statutes
    and do not keep my commandments;

I will punish their transgressions with a rod
    and their iniquities with the lash;

But I will not take my love from him,
    nor let my faithfulness prove false.

I will not break my covenant,
    nor change what has gone out of my lips.

Once for all I have sworn by my holiness:
    'I will not lie to David.

His line shall endure for ever
    and his throne as the sun before me;

It shall stand fast for evermore like the moon,
    the abiding witness in the sky.'"

But you have cast off and rejected your anointed;
    you have become enraged at him.

You have broken your covenant with your servant,
    defiled his crown, and hurled it to the ground.

You have breached all his walls
    and laid his strongholds in ruins.

All who pass by despoil him;
    he has become the scorn of his neighbors.

You have exalted the right hand of his foes
    and made all his enemies rejoice.

You have turned back the edge of his sword
    and have not sustained him in battle.

You have put an end to his splendor
    and cast his throne to the ground.

You have cut short the days of his youth
    and have covered him with shame.

How long will you hide yourself, O LORD?
will you hide yourself for ever?
    how long will your anger burn like fire?

Remember, LORD, how short life is,
    how frail you have made all flesh.

Who can live and not see death?
  who can save himself from the power of the grave?

Where, Lord, are your loving-kindnesses of old,
  which you promised David in your faithfulness?

Remember, Lord, how your servant is mocked,
  how I carry in my bosom the taunts of many peoples,

The taunts your enemies have hurled, O LORD,
  which they hurled at the heels of your anointed.

Blessed be the LORD for evermore!
  Amen, I say, Amen.

PSALM 114

Hallelujah!
When Israel came out of Egypt,
  the house of Jacob from a people of strange speech,

Judah became God's sanctuary
  and Israel his dominion.

The sea beheld it and fled;
  Jordan turned and went back.

The mountains skipped like rams,
  and the little hills like young sheep.

What ailed you, O sea, that you fled?
  O Jordan, that you turned back?

You mountains, that you skipped like rams?
  you little hills like young sheep?

Tremble, O earth, at the presence of the Lord,
  at the presence of the God of Jacob,

Who turned the hard rock into a pool of water
and flint-stone into a flowing spring.

✐ PSALM 115

Not to us, O LORD, not to us,
but to your Name give glory;
because of your love and because of your faithfulness.

Why should the heathen say,
"Where then is their God?"

Our God is in heaven;
whatever he wills to do he does.

Their idols are silver and gold,
the work of human hands.

They have mouths, but they cannot speak;
eyes have they, but they cannot see;

They have ears, but they cannot hear;
noses, but they cannot smell;

They have hands, but they cannot feel;
feet, but they cannot walk;
they make no sound with their throat.

Those who make them are like them,
and so are all who put their trust in them.

O Israel, trust in the LORD;
he is their help and their shield.

O house of Aaron, trust in the LORD;
he is their help and their shield.

You who fear the LORD, trust in the LORD;
he is their help and their shield.

The LORD has been mindful of us, and he will bless us;
>   he will bless the house of Israel;
>   he will bless the house of Aaron;

He will bless those who fear the LORD,
>   both small and great together.

May the LORD increase you more and more,
>   you and your children after you.

May you be blessed by the LORD,
>   the maker of heaven and earth.

The heaven of heavens is the LORD's,
>   but he entrusted the earth to its peoples.

The dead do not praise the LORD,
>   nor all those who go down into silence;

But we will bless the LORD,
>   from this time forth for evermore.
>   Hallelujah!

⟋ PSALM 45

Understanding this same Word to be the Son of God, the Psalter sings
Psalm 45 in the voice of the Father: "My heart has belched a good
Word."*

My heart is stirring with a noble song;
let me recite what I have fashioned for the king;
>   my tongue shall be the pen of a skilled writer.

You are the fairest of men;
>   grace flows from your lips,
>   because God has blessed you for ever.

---

*Athanasius's version of the LXX 44:2 (45:1 BCP) reads: Ἐξηρεύξατο ἡ καρδία μου Λόγον
ἀγαθόν. See Athanasius, *Epistola ad Marcellinum*, PG 27:13d.

Strap your sword upon your thigh, O mighty warrior,
    in your pride and in your majesty.

Ride out and conquer in the cause of truth
    and for the sake of justice.

Your right hand will show you marvelous things;
    your arrows are very sharp, O mighty warrior.

The peoples are falling at your feet,
    and the king's enemies are losing heart.

Your throne, O God, endures for ever and ever,
    a scepter of righteousness is the scepter of your kingdom;
    you love righteousness and hate iniquity.

Therefore God, your God, has anointed you
    with the oil of gladness above your fellows.

All your garments are fragrant with myrrh, aloes, and cassia,
    and the music of strings from ivory palaces makes you glad.

Kings' daughters stand among the ladies of the court;
    on your right hand is the queen,
    adorned with the gold of Ophir.

"Hear, O daughter; consider and listen closely;
    forget your people and your father's house.

The king will have pleasure in your beauty;
    he is your master; therefore do him honor.

The people of Tyre are here with a gift;
    the rich among the people seek your favor."

All glorious is the princess as she enters;
    her gown is cloth-of-gold.

In embroidered apparel she is brought to the king;
    after her the bridesmaids follow in procession.

With joy and gladness they are brought,
    and enter into the palace of the king.

"In place of fathers, O king, you shall have sons;
    you shall make them princes over all the earth.

I will make your name to be remembered
from one generation to another;
    therefore nations will praise you for ever and ever."

⟋⟋ PSALM 47

Psalms 24 and 47 relate the Savior's ascension into heaven.

Clap your hands, all you peoples;
    shout to God with a cry of joy.

For the LORD Most High is to be feared;
    he is the great King over all the earth.

He subdues the peoples under us,
    and the nations under our feet.

He chooses our inheritance for us,
    the pride of Jacob whom he loves.

God has gone up with a shout,
    the LORD with the sound of the ram's-horn.

Sing praises to God, sing praises;
    sing praises to our King, sing praises.

For God is King of all the earth;
    sing praises with all your skill.

God reigns over the nations;
    God sits upon his holy throne.

The nobles of the peoples have gathered together
    with the people of the God of Abraham.

The rulers of the earth belong to God,
    and he is highly exalted.

～ PSALM 50

Psalm 50 affirms the coming of the Savior and that as God, he will
come among us.

The LORD, the God of gods, has spoken;
    he has called the earth from the rising of the sun to
        its setting.

Out of Zion, perfect in its beauty,
    God reveals himself in glory.

Our God will come and will not keep silence;
    before him there is a consuming flame,
    and round about him a raging storm.

He calls the heavens and the earth from above
    to witness the judgment of his people.

"Gather before me my loyal followers,
    those who have made a covenant with me
    and sealed it with sacrifice."

Let the heavens declare the rightness of his cause;
    for God himself is judge.

Hear, O my people, and I will speak:
"O Israel, I will bear witness against you;
    for I am God, your God.

I do not accuse you because of your sacrifices;
    your offerings are always before me.

I will take no bull-calf from your stalls,
    nor he-goats out of your pens;

For all the beasts of the forest are mine,
the herds in their thousands upon the hills.

I know every bird in the sky,
and the creatures of the fields are in my sight.

If I were hungry, I would not tell you,
for the whole world is mine and all that is in it.

Do you think I eat the flesh of bulls,
or drink the blood of goats?

Offer to God a sacrifice of thanksgiving
and make good your vows to the Most High.

Call upon me in the day of trouble;
I will deliver you, and you shall honor me."

But to the wicked God says:
"Why do you recite my statutes,
and take my covenant upon your lips;

Since you refuse discipline,
and toss my words behind your back?

When you see a thief, you make him your friend,
and you cast in your lot with adulterers.

You have loosed your lips for evil,
and harnessed your tongue to a lie.

You are always speaking evil of your brother
and slandering your own mother's son.

These things you have done, and I kept still,
and you thought that I am like you."

"I have made my accusation;
I have put my case in order before your eyes.

Consider this well, you who forget God,
    lest I rend you and there be none to deliver you.

Whoever offers me the sacrifice of thanksgiving
              honors me;
    but to those who keep in my way will I show
              the salvation of God."

⌒ PSALM 99

When you read Psalms 93, 96, 98, and 99 you can perceive the wonderful deeds performed by the Savior for us through his sufferings.

The LORD is King;
let the people tremble;
    he is enthroned upon the cherubim;
    let the earth shake.

The LORD is great in Zion;
    he is high above all peoples.

Let them confess his Name, which is great and awesome;
    he is the Holy One.

"O mighty King, lover of justice,
you have established equity;
    you have executed justice and righteousness in Jacob."

Proclaim the greatness of the LORD our God
and fall down before his footstool;
    he is the Holy One.

Moses and Aaron among his priests,
and Samuel among those who call upon his Name,
    they called upon the LORD, and he answered them.

He spoke to them out of the pillar of cloud;
    they kept his testimonies and the decree that he gave them.

"O LORD our God, you answered them indeed;
you were a God who forgave them,
yet punished them for their evil deeds."

Proclaim the greatness of the LORD our God
and worship him upon his holy hill;
for the LORD our God is the Holy One.

PSALM 110

When you want to sing something concerning the Savior, you find such references in nearly every psalm. But you have especially Psalms 45 and 110, which make known his actual generation from the Father and his coming in the flesh.

The LORD said to my Lord, "Sit at my right hand,
until I make your enemies your footstool."

The LORD will send the scepter of your power out of Zion,
saying, "Rule over your enemies round about you.

Princely state has been yours from the day of your birth;
in the beauty of holiness have I begotten you,
like dew from the womb of the morning."

The LORD has sworn and he will not recant:
"You are a priest for ever after the order of Melchizedek."

The Lord who is at your right hand
will smite kings in the day of his wrath;
he will rule over the nations.

He will heap high the corpses;
he will smash heads over the wide earth.

He will drink from the brook beside the road;
therefore he will lift high his head.

SEVEN

Psalms for Instruction

PSALMS 1, 112, AND 128

If you want to bless someone, you learn how to do so, whom to address, and the words to say in Psalms 1, 32, 41, 112, 119, and 128.

∽ PSALM 1

Happy are they who have not walked in the counsel of
the wicked,
nor lingered in the way of sinners,
nor sat in the seats of the scornful!

Their delight is in the law of the LORD,
and they meditate on his law day and night.

They are like trees planted by streams of water,
bearing fruit in due season, with leaves that do not wither;
everything they do shall prosper.

It is not so with the wicked;
they are like chaff which the wind blows away.

Therefore the wicked shall not stand upright when
judgment comes,
nor the sinner in the council of the righteous.

For the LORD knows the way of the righteous,
but the way of the wicked is doomed.

∾ PSALM 112

Hallelujah!
Happy are they who fear the Lord
and have great delight in his commandments!

Their descendants will be mighty in the land;
the generation of the upright will be blessed.

Wealth and riches will be in their house,
and their righteousness will last for ever.

Light shines in the darkness for the upright;
the righteous are merciful and full of compassion.

It is good for them to be generous in lending
and to manage their affairs with justice.

For they will never be shaken;
the righteous will be kept in everlasting remembrance.

They will not be afraid of any evil rumors;
their heart is right;
they put their trust in the Lord.

Their heart is established and will not shrink,
until they see their desire upon their enemies.

They have given freely to the poor,
and their righteousness stands fast for ever;
they will hold up their head with honor.

The wicked will see it and be angry;
they will gnash their teeth and pine away;
the desires of the wicked will perish.

∽ PSALM 128

Happy are they all who fear the LORD,
   and who follow in his ways!

You shall eat the fruit of your labor;
   happiness and prosperity shall be yours.

Your wife shall be like a fruitful vine within your house,
   your children like olive shoots round about your table.

The man who fears the LORD
   shall thus indeed be blessed.

The LORD bless you from Zion,
   and may you see the prosperity of Jerusalem all the days
      of your life.

May you live to see your children's children;
   may peace be upon Israel.

∽ PSALM 15

If you want to learn what a citizen of the kingdom of heaven is like,
sing Psalm 15.

LORD, who may dwell in your tabernacle?
   who may abide upon your holy hill?

Whoever leads a blameless life and does what is right,
   who speaks the truth from his heart.

There is no guile upon his tongue;
he does no evil to his friend;
   he does not heap contempt upon his neighbor.

In his sight the wicked is rejected,
   but he honors those who fear the LORD.

He has sworn to do no wrong
    and does not take back his word.

He does not give his money in hope of gain,
    nor does he take a bribe against the innocent.

Whoever does these things
    shall never be overthrown.

☙ PSALM 29

If while giving thanks you want to learn how to make an offering to the
Lord, sing Psalm 29 with spiritual understanding.

Ascribe to the LORD, you gods,
    ascribe to the LORD glory and strength.

Ascribe to the LORD the glory due his Name;
    worship the LORD in the beauty of holiness.

The voice of the LORD is upon the waters;
the God of glory thunders;
    the LORD is upon the mighty waters.

The voice of the LORD is a powerful voice;
    the voice of the LORD is a voice of splendor.

The voice of the LORD breaks the cedar trees;
    the LORD breaks the cedars of Lebanon;

He makes Lebanon skip like a calf,
    and Mount Hermon like a young wild ox.

The voice of the LORD splits the flames of fire;
the voice of the LORD shakes the wilderness;
    the LORD shakes the wilderness of Kadesh.

The voice of the LORD makes the oak trees writhe
    and strips the forests bare.

And in the temple of the Lord
   all are crying, "Glory!"

The LORD sits enthroned above the flood;
   the LORD sits enthroned as King for evermore.

The LORD shall give strength to his people;
   the LORD shall give his people the blessing of peace.

PSALMS 30 AND 127

When dedicating your house—which means to welcome the Lord both in your soul and in the material place where you live—give thanks and say Psalm 30 and 127, which is among the Psalms of Ascent.

ᴄᵔ PSALM 30

I will exalt you, O LORD,
because you have lifted me up
   and have not let my enemies triumph over me.

O LORD my God, I cried out to you,
   and you restored me to health.

You brought me up, O LORD, from the dead;
   you restored my life as I was going down to the grave.

Sing to the LORD, you servants of his;
   give thanks for the remembrance of his holiness.

For his wrath endures but the twinkling of an eye,
   his favor for a lifetime.

Weeping may spend the night,
   but joy comes in the morning.

While I felt secure, I said,
"I shall never be disturbed.
   You, LORD, with your favor, made me as strong as
      the mountains."

Then you hid your face,
    and I was filled with fear.

I cried to you, O LORD;
    I pleaded with the Lord, saying,

"What profit is there in my blood, if I go down to the Pit?
    will the dust praise you or declare your faithfulness?

Hear, O LORD, and have mercy upon me;
    O LORD, be my helper."

You have turned my wailing into dancing;
    you have put off my sack-cloth and clothed me with joy.

Therefore my heart sings to you without ceasing;
    O LORD my God, I will give you thanks for ever.

～ PSALM 127

Unless the LORD builds the house,
    their labor is in vain who build it.

Unless the LORD watches over the city,
    in vain the watchman keeps his vigil.

It is in vain that you rise so early and go to bed so late;
    vain, too, to eat the bread of toil,
    for he gives to his beloved sleep.

Children are a heritage from the LORD,
    and the fruit of the womb is a gift.

Like arrows in the hand of a warrior
    are the children of one's youth.

Happy is the man who has his quiver full of them!
    he shall not be put to shame
        when he contends with his enemies in the gate.

⌒⌒ PSALM 36

If you know people who break the law and delight in their rebellious behavior, do not attribute the evil in them to nature. That is what the heretics say. Instead, say Psalm 36 and you will see that they are to blame for their sinning.

There is a voice of rebellion deep in the heart of the wicked;
    there is no fear of God before his eyes.

He flatters himself in his own eyes
    that his hateful sin will not be found out.

The words of his mouth are wicked and deceitful;
    he has left off acting wisely and doing good.

He thinks up wickedness upon his bed
and has set himself in no good way;
    he does not abhor that which is evil.

Your love, O LORD, reaches to the heavens,
    and your faithfulness to the clouds.

Your righteousness is like the strong mountains,
your justice like the great deep;
    you save both man and beast, O LORD.

How priceless is your love, O God!
    your people take refuge under the
        shadow of your wings.

They feast upon the abundance of your house;
    you give them drink from the river of your delights.

For with you is the well of life,
    and in your light we see light.

Continue your loving-kindness to those who know you,
    and your favor to those who are true of heart.

Let not the foot of the proud come near me,
  nor the hand of the wicked push me aside.

See how they are fallen, those who work wickedness!
  they are cast down and shall not be able to rise.

～ PSALM 41

When you see people who are poor and in need, and you want to be
generous to them, you can affirm those who have already shown them
mercy while encouraging others to do the same by saying Psalm 41.

Happy are they who consider the poor and needy!
  the LORD will deliver them in the time of trouble.

The LORD preserves them and keeps them alive,
so that they may be happy in the land;
  he does not hand them over to the will of their enemies.

The LORD sustains them on their sickbed
  and ministers to them in their illness.

I said, "LORD, be merciful to me;
  heal me, for I have sinned against you."

My enemies are saying wicked things about me:
  "When will he die, and his name perish?"

Even if they come to see me, they speak empty words;
  their heart collects false rumors;
  they go outside and spread them.

All my enemies whisper together about me
  and devise evil against me.

"A deadly thing," they say, "has fastened on him;
  he has taken to his bed and will never get up again."

Even my best friend, whom I trusted,
who broke bread with me,
  has lifted up his heel and turned against me.

But you, O LORD, be merciful to me and raise me up,
  and I shall repay them.

By this I know you are pleased with me,
  that my enemy does not triumph over me.

In my integrity you hold me fast,
  and shall set me before your face for ever.

Blessed be the LORD God of Israel,
  from age to age. Amen. Amen.

∽ PSALM 66

If you want to teach people about the resurrection, sing the words in
Psalm 66.

Be joyful in God, all you lands;
  sing the glory of his Name;
  sing the glory of his praise.

Say to God, "How awesome are your deeds!
  because of your great strength your enemies
    cringe before you.

All the earth bows down before you,
  sings to you, sings out your Name."

Come now and see the works of God,
  how wonderful he is in his doing toward all people.

He turned the sea into dry land,
so that they went through the water on foot,
  and there we rejoiced in him.

In his might he rules for ever;
his eyes keep watch over the nations;
   let no rebel rise up against him.

Bless our God, you peoples;
   make the voice of his praise to be heard;

Who holds our souls in life,
   and will not allow our feet to slip.

For you, O God, have proved us;
   you have tried us just as silver is tried.

You brought us into the snare;
   you laid heavy burdens upon our backs.

You let enemies ride over our heads;
we went through fire and water;
   but you brought us out into a place of refreshment.

I will enter your house with burnt-offerings
and will pay you my vows,
   which I promised with my lips
   and spoke with my mouth when I was in trouble.

I will offer you sacrifices of fat beasts
with the smoke of rams;
   I will give you oxen and goats.

Come and listen, all you who fear God,
   and I will tell you what he has done for me.

I called out to him with my mouth,
   and his praise was on my tongue.

If I had found evil in my heart,
   the Lord would not have heard me;

But in truth God has heard me;
   he has attended to the voice of my prayer.

Blessed be God, who has not rejected my prayer,
>   nor withheld his love from me.

∽ PSALM 76

When you want to convince pagans and heretics that the knowledge of God is not with them but only in the catholic church, you can sing and say with understanding the words in Psalm 76.

In Judah is God known;
>   his Name is great in Israel.

At Salem is his tabernacle,
>   and his dwelling is in Zion.

There he broke the flashing arrows,
>   the shield, the sword, and the weapons of battle.

How glorious you are!
>   more splendid than the everlasting mountains!

The strong of heart have been despoiled;
they sink into sleep;
>   none of the warriors can lift a hand.

At your rebuke, O God of Jacob,
>   both horse and rider lie stunned.

What terror you inspire!
>   who can stand before you when you are angry?

From heaven you pronounced judgment;
>   the earth was afraid and was still;

When God rose up to judgment
>   and to save all the oppressed of the earth.

Truly, wrathful Edom will give you thanks,
>   and the remnant of Hamath will keep your feasts.

Make a vow to the LORD your God and keep it;
   let all around him bring gifts to him who is worthy
      to be feared.

He breaks the spirit of princes,
   and strikes terror in the kings of the earth.

⌒ PSALM 87

If you want to know the difference between the catholic church and the
schismatic groups, and so persuade the latter, you can say the words
written in Psalm 87.

On the holy mountain stands the city he has founded;
   the LORD loves the gates of Zion
   more than all the dwellings of Jacob.

Glorious things are spoken of you,
   O city of our God.

I count Egypt and Babylon among those who know me;
   behold Philistia, Tyre, and Ethiopia:
   in Zion were they born.

Of Zion it shall be said, "Everyone was born in her,
   and the Most High himself shall sustain her."

The LORD will record as he enrolls the peoples,
   "These also were born there."

The singers and the dancers will say,
   "All my fresh springs are in you."

∾ PSALM 90

If you want to learn how Moses prayed, you have Psalm 90.

Lord, you have been our refuge
    from one generation to another.

Before the mountains were brought forth,
or the land and the earth were born,
    from age to age you are God.

You turn us back to the dust and say,
    "Go back, O child of earth."

For a thousand years in your sight are like yesterday
        when it is past
    and like a watch in the night.

You sweep us away like a dream;
    we fade away suddenly like the grass.

In the morning it is green and flourishes;
    in the evening it is dried up and withered.

For we consume away in your displeasure;
    we are afraid because of your wrathful indignation.

Our iniquities you have set before you,
    and our secret sins in the light of your countenance.

When you are angry, all our days are gone;
    we bring our years to an end like a sigh.

The span of our life is seventy years,
perhaps in strength even eighty;
    yet the sum of them is but labor and sorrow,
    for they pass away quickly and we are gone.

Who regards the power of your wrath?
    who rightly fears your indignation?

So teach us to number our days
   that we may apply our hearts to wisdom.

Return, O LORD; how long will you tarry?
   be gracious to your servants.

Satisfy us by your loving-kindness in the morning;
   so shall we rejoice and be glad all the days of our life.

Make us glad by the measure of the days that you afflicted us
   and the years in which we suffered adversity.

Show your servants your works
   and your splendor to their children.

May the graciousness of the LORD our God be upon us;
   prosper the work of our hands;
   prosper our handiwork.

∽ PSALM 100

When you see the Lord's authority and providence in all things and you
want to teach others to trust and obey him, persuade them first to give
thanks by singing Psalm 100.

Be joyful in the LORD, all you lands;
   serve the LORD with gladness
   and come before his presence with a song.

Know this: The LORD himself is God;
   he himself has made us, and we are his;
   we are his people and the sheep of his pasture.

Enter his gates with thanksgiving;
go into his courts with praise;
   give thanks to him and call upon his Name.

For the LORD is good;
his mercy is everlasting;
    and his faithfulness endures from age to age.

ᴖ PSALM 101

When you learn of his just rule, that the Lord makes a decision by
mixing judgment with mercy, if you want to come before him, you have
the words in Psalm 101.

I will sing of mercy and justice;
    to you, O LORD, will I sing praises.

I will strive to follow a blameless course;
oh, when will you come to me?
    I will walk with sincerity of heart within my house.

I will set no worthless thing before my eyes;
    I hate the doers of evil deeds;
    they shall not remain with me.

A crooked heart shall be far from me;
    I will not know evil.

Those who in secret slander their neighbors I will destroy;
    those who have a haughty look and a proud
        heart I cannot abide.

My eyes are upon the faithful in the land, that they may
        dwell with me,
    and only those who lead a blameless life shall
        be my servants.

Those who act deceitfully shall not dwell in my house,
    and those who tell lies shall not continue in my sight.

I will soon destroy all the wicked in the land,
    that I may root out all evildoers from the city of the LORD.

PSALMS 107, 135, 147, 148, AND 150*

Do you want to praise God, and to know how and for what one should praise, and what words are fitting to speak the praise? You have Psalms 105, 107, 135, 146, 147, 148, and 150.

⌒ PSALM 107

Give thanks to the LORD, for he is good,
and his mercy endures for ever.

Let all those whom the LORD has redeemed proclaim
that he redeemed them from the hand of the foe.

He gathered them out of the lands;
from the east and from the west,
from the north and from the south.

Some wandered in desert wastes;
they found no way to a city where they might dwell.

They were hungry and thirsty;
their spirits languished within them.

Then they cried to the LORD in their trouble,
and he delivered them from their distress.

He put their feet on a straight path
to go to a city where they might dwell.

Let them give thanks to the LORD for his mercy
and the wonders he does for his children.

For he satisfies the thirsty
and fills the hungry with good things.

Some sat in darkness and deep gloom,
bound fast in misery and iron;

---

* The reader will note that Psalms 146 and 147 in Athanasius's LXX are the equivalent of Psalms 147:1–12 and 147:13–21 in the BCP (here I have included the full Psalm 147 in the BCP).

Because they rebelled against the words of God
    and despised the counsel of the Most High.

So he humbled their spirits with hard labor;
    they stumbled, and there was none to help.

Then they cried to the LORD in their trouble,
    and he delivered them from their distress.

He led them out of darkness and deep gloom
    and broke their bonds asunder.

Let them give thanks to the LORD for his mercy
    and the wonders he does for his children.

For he shatters the doors of bronze
    and breaks in two the iron bars.

Some were fools and took to rebellious ways;
    they were afflicted because of their sins.

They abhorred all manner of food
    and drew near to death's door.

Then they cried to the LORD in their trouble,
    and he delivered them from their distress.

He sent forth his word and healed them
    and saved them from the grave.

Let them give thanks to the LORD for his mercy
    and the wonders he does for his children.

Let them offer a sacrifice of thanksgiving
    and tell of his acts with shouts of joy.

Some went down to the sea in ships
    and plied their trade in deep waters;

They beheld the works of the LORD
    and his wonders in the deep.

Then he spoke, and a stormy wind arose,
　　which tossed high the waves of the sea.

They mounted up to the heavens and fell back to the depths;
　　their hearts melted because of their peril.

They reeled and staggered like drunkards
　　and were at their wits' end.

Then they cried to the LORD in their trouble,
　　and he delivered them from their distress.

He stilled the storm to a whisper
　　and quieted the waves of the sea.

Then were they glad because of the calm,
　　and he brought them to the harbor they were bound for.

Let them give thanks to the LORD for his mercy
　　and the wonders he does for his children.

Let them exalt him in the congregation of the people
　　and praise him in the council of the elders.

The LORD changed rivers into deserts,
　　and water-springs into thirsty ground,

A fruitful land into salt flats,
　　because of the wickedness of those who dwell there.

He changed deserts into pools of water
　　and dry land into water-springs.

He settled the hungry there,
　　and they founded a city to dwell in.

They sowed fields, and planted vineyards,
　　and brought in a fruitful harvest.

He blessed them, so that they increased greatly;
　　he did not let their herds decrease.

Yet when they were diminished and brought low,
    through stress of adversity and sorrow,

(He pours contempt on princes
    and makes them wander in trackless wastes)

He lifted up the poor out of misery
    and multiplied their families like flocks of sheep.

The upright will see this and rejoice,
    but all wickedness will shut its mouth.

Whoever is wise will ponder these things,
    and consider well the mercies of the LORD.

⌒ PSALM 135

Hallelujah!
Praise the Name of the LORD;
    give praise, you servants of the LORD,

You who stand in the house of the LORD,
    in the courts of the house of our God.

Praise the LORD, for the LORD is good;
    sing praises to his Name, for it is lovely.

For the LORD has chosen Jacob for himself
    and Israel for his own possession.

For I know that the LORD is great,
    and that our Lord is above all gods.

The LORD does whatever pleases him, in heaven and on earth,
    in the seas and all the deeps.

He brings up rain clouds from the ends of the earth;
    he sends out lightning with the rain,
    and brings the winds out of his storehouse.

It was he who struck down the firstborn of Egypt,
    the firstborn both of man and beast.

He sent signs and wonders into the midst of you, O Egypt,
    against Pharaoh and all his servants.

He overthrew many nations
    and put mighty kings to death:

Sihon, king of the Amorites,
and Og, the king of Bashan,
    and all the kingdoms of Canaan.

He gave their land to be an inheritance,
    an inheritance for Israel his people.

O LORD, your Name is everlasting;
    your renown, O LORD, endures from age to age.

For the LORD gives his people justice
    and shows compassion to his servants.

The idols of the heathen are silver and gold,
    the work of human hands.

They have mouths, but they cannot speak;
    eyes have they, but they cannot see.

They have ears, but they cannot hear;
    neither is there any breath in their mouth.

Those who make them are like them,
    and so are all who put their trust in them.

Bless the LORD, O house of Israel;
    O house of Aaron, bless the LORD.

Bless the LORD, O house of Levi;
    you who fear the LORD, bless the LORD.

Blessed be the LORD out of Zion,
  who dwells in Jerusalem.
  Hallelujah!

⌒ PSALM 147

Hallelujah!
How good it is to sing praises to our God!
  how pleasant it is to honor him with praise!

The LORD rebuilds Jerusalem;
  he gathers the exiles of Israel.

He heals the brokenhearted
  and binds up their wounds.

He counts the number of the stars
  and calls them all by their names.

Great is our LORD and mighty in power;
  there is no limit to his wisdom.

The LORD lifts up the lowly,
  but casts the wicked to the ground.

Sing to the LORD with thanksgiving;
  make music to our God upon the harp.

He covers the heavens with clouds
  and prepares rain for the earth;

He makes grass to grow upon the mountains
  and green plants to serve mankind.

He provides food for flocks and herds
  and for the young ravens when they cry.

He is not impressed by the might of a horse;
  he has no pleasure in the strength of a man;

But the LORD has pleasure in those who fear him,
    in those who await his gracious favor.

Worship the LORD, O Jerusalem;
    praise your God, O Zion;

For he has strengthened the bars of your gates;
    he has blessed your children within you.

He has established peace on your borders;
    he satisfies you with the finest wheat.

He sends out his command to the earth,
    and his word runs very swiftly.

He gives snow like wool;
    he scatters hoarfrost like ashes.

He scatters his hail like bread crumbs;
    who can stand against his cold?

He sends forth his word and melts them;
    he blows with his wind, and the waters flow.

He declares his word to Jacob,
    his statutes and his judgments to Israel.

He has not done so to any other nation;
    to them he has not revealed his judgments.
    Hallelujah!

～ PSALM 148

Hallelujah!
Praise the LORD from the heavens;
    praise him in the heights.

Praise him, all you angels of his;
    praise him, all his host.

Praise him, sun and moon;
    praise him, all you shining stars.

Praise him, heaven of heavens,
    and you waters above the heavens.

Let them praise the Name of the LORD;
    for he commanded, and they were created.

He made them stand fast for ever and ever;
    he gave them a law which shall not pass away.

Praise the LORD from the earth,
    you sea-monsters and all deeps;

Fire and hail, snow and fog,
    tempestuous wind, doing his will;

Mountains and all hills,
    fruit trees and all cedars;

Wild beasts and all cattle,
    creeping things and wingèd birds;

Kings of the earth and all peoples,
    princes and all rulers of the world;

Young men and maidens,
    old and young together.

Let them praise the Name of the LORD,
    for his Name only is exalted,
    his splendor is over earth and heaven.

He has raised up strength for his people
and praise for all his loyal servants,
    the children of Israel, a people who are near him.
    Hallelujah!

PSALM 150

Hallelujah!
Praise God in his holy temple;
  praise him in the firmament of his power.
Praise him for his mighty acts;
  praise him for his excellent greatness.

Praise him with the blast of the ram's-horn;
  praise him with lyre and harp.

Praise him with timbrel and dance;
  praise him with strings and pipe.

Praise him with resounding cymbals;
  praise him with loud-clanging cymbals.

Let everything that has breath
praise the Lord.
  Hallelujah!

EIGHT

Psalms for Daily Life

∽ PSALM 24

Do you want to give thanks on Sunday? Study carefully Psalm 24.

The earth is the LORD'S and all that is in it,
　　the world and all who dwell therein.

For it is he who founded it upon the seas
　　and made it firm upon the rivers of the deep.

"Who can ascend the hill of the LORD?
　　and who can stand in his holy place?"

"Those who have clean hands and a pure heart,
　　who have not pledged themselves to falsehood,
　　　　nor sworn by what is a fraud.

They shall receive a blessing from the Lord
　　and a just reward from the God of their salvation."

Such is the generation of those who seek him,
　　of those who seek your face, O God of Jacob.

Lift up your heads, O gates;
lift them high, O everlasting doors;
　　and the King of glory shall come in.

"Who is this King of glory?"
　　"The LORD, strong and mighty,
　　the LORD, mighty in battle."

Lift up your heads, O gates;
lift them high, O everlasting doors;
　　and the King of glory shall come in.

"Who is he, this King of glory?"
   "The LORD of hosts,
   he is the King of glory."

⌁ PSALM 33

Whenever you want to sing with a group, getting together with people
who are honest and faithful in life, say with them Psalm 33.

Rejoice in the LORD, you righteous;
   it is good for the just to sing praises.

Praise the LORD with the harp;
   play to him upon the psaltery and lyre.

Sing for him a new song;
   sound a fanfare with all your skill upon the trumpet.

For the word of the LORD is right,
   and all his works are sure.

He loves righteousness and justice;
   the loving-kindness of the LORD fills the whole earth.

By the word of the LORD were the heavens made,
   by the breath of his mouth all the heavenly hosts.

He gathers up the waters of the ocean as in a water-skin
   and stores up the depths of the sea.

Let all the earth fear the LORD;
   let all who dwell in the world stand in awe of him.

For he spoke, and it came to pass;
   he commanded, and it stood fast.

The LORD brings the will of the nations to naught;
   he thwarts the designs of the peoples.

But the LORD's will stands fast for ever,
    and the designs of his heart from age to age.

Happy is the nation whose God is the LORD!
    happy the people he has chosen to be his own!

The LORD looks down from heaven,
    and beholds all the people in the world.

From where he sits enthroned he turns his gaze
    on all who dwell on the earth.

He fashions all the hearts of them
    and understands all their works.

There is no king that can be saved by a mighty army;
    a strong man is not delivered by his great strength.

The horse is a vain hope for deliverance;
    for all its strength it cannot save.

Behold, the eye of the LORD is upon those who fear him,
    on those who wait upon his love,

To pluck their lives from death,
    and to feed them in time of famine.

Our soul waits for the LORD;
    he is our help and our shield.

Indeed, our heart rejoices in him,
    for in his holy Name we put our trust.

Let your loving-kindness, O LORD, be upon us,
    as we have put our trust in you.

☙ PSALM 48

Do you want to sing praises to God on Monday? Say the words in
Psalm 48.

Great is the LORD, and highly to be praised;
    in the city of our God is his holy hill.

Beautiful and lofty, the joy of all the earth, is the
        hill of Zion,
    the very center of the world and the city of the great King.

God is in her citadels;
    he is known to be her sure refuge.

Behold, the kings of the earth assembled
    and marched forward together.

They looked and were astounded;
    they retreated and fled in terror.

Trembling seized them there;
    they writhed like a woman in childbirth,
    like ships of the sea when the east wind shatters them.

As we have heard, so have we seen,
in the city of the LORD of hosts, in the city of our God;
    God has established her for ever.

We have waited in silence on your loving-kindness, O God,
    in the midst of your temple.

Your praise, like your Name, O God, reaches to
        the world's end;
    your right hand is full of justice.

Let Mount Zion be glad
and the cities of Judah rejoice,
    because of your judgments.

Make the circuit of Zion;
walk round about her;
> count the number of her towers.

Consider well her bulwarks;
examine her strongholds;
> that you may tell those who come after.

This God is our God for ever and ever;
> he shall be our guide for evermore.

PSALMS 81 AND 95

If you want to praise the Lord on a feast day, get together with the servants of God and sing the words in Psalms 81 and 95.

∽ PSALM 81

Sing with joy to God our strength
> and raise a loud shout to the God of Jacob.

Raise a song and sound the timbrel,
> the merry harp, and the lyre.

Blow the ram's-horn at the new moon,
> and at the full moon, the day of our feast.

For this is a statute for Israel,
> a law of the God of Jacob.

He laid it as a solemn charge upon Joseph,
> when he came out of the land of Egypt.

I heard an unfamiliar voice saying,
> "I eased his shoulder from the burden;
> his hands were set free from bearing the load."

You called on me in trouble, and I saved you;
    I answered you from the secret place of thunder
    and tested you at the waters of Meribah.

Hear, O my people, and I will admonish you:
    O Israel, if you would but listen to me!

There shall be no strange god among you;
    you shall not worship a foreign god.

I am the LORD your God,
who brought you out of the land of Egypt and said,
    "Open your mouth wide, and I will fill it."

And yet my people did not hear my voice,
    and Israel would not obey me.

So I gave them over to the stubbornness of their hearts,
    to follow their own devices.

Oh, that my people would listen to me!
    that Israel would walk in my ways!

I should soon subdue their enemies
    and turn my hand against their foes.

Those who hate the LORD would cringe before him,
    and their punishment would last for ever.

But Israel would I feed with the finest wheat
    and satisfy him with honey from the rock.

⌒ PSALM 95

Come, let us sing to the LORD;
    let us shout for joy to the Rock of our salvation.

Let us come before his presence with thanksgiving
    and raise a loud shout to him with psalms.

For the LORD is a great God,
>and a great King above all gods.

In his hand are the caverns of the earth,
>and the heights of the hills are his also.

The sea is his, for he made it,
>and his hands have molded the dry land.

Come, let us bow down, and bend the knee,
>and kneel before the LORD our Maker.

For he is our God,
and we are the people of his pasture and the sheep of his hand.
>Oh, that today you would hearken to his voice!

Harden not your hearts,
as your forebears did in the wilderness,
>at Meribah, and on that day at Massah,
>when they tempted me.

They put me to the test,
>though they had seen my works.

Forty years long I detested that generation and said,
>"This people are wayward in their hearts;
>they do not know my ways."

So I swore in my wrath,
>"They shall not enter into my rest."

ﾟ PSALM 84

If while seeing the house of God and its eternal courts you have a deep
longing for these things like the Apostle had, say also Psalm 84.

How dear to me is your dwelling, O LORD of hosts!
>My soul has a desire and longing for the courts of the LORD;
>my heart and my flesh rejoice in the living God.

The sparrow has found her a house
and the swallow a nest where she may lay her young;
 by the side of your altars, O LORD of hosts,
 my King and my God.

Happy are they who dwell in your house!
 they will always be praising you.

Happy are the people whose strength is in you!
 whose hearts are set on the pilgrims' way.

Those who go through the desolate valley will find
   it a place of springs,
 for the early rains have covered it with pools of water.

They will climb from height to height,
 and the God of gods will reveal himself in Zion.

LORD God of hosts, hear my prayer;
 hearken, O God of Jacob.

Behold our defender, O God;
 and look upon the face of your Anointed.

For one day in your courts is better than
   a thousand in my own room,
 and to stand at the threshold of the house of my God
 than to dwell in the tents of the wicked.

For the LORD God is both sun and shield;
 he will give grace and glory;

No good thing will the LORD withhold
 from those who walk with integrity.

O LORD of hosts,
 happy are they who put their trust in you!

⌒ PSALM 92

Do you want to sing praises on Saturday? You have Psalm 92.

It is a good thing to give thanks to the LORD,
    and to sing praises to your Name, O Most High;

To tell of your loving-kindness early in the morning
    and of your faithfulness in the night season;

On the psaltery, and on the lyre,
    and to the melody of the harp.

For you have made me glad by your acts, O LORD;
    and I shout for joy because of the works of your hands.

LORD, how great are your works!
    your thoughts are very deep.

The dullard does not know,
nor does the fool understand,
        that though the wicked grow like weeds,
        and all the workers of iniquity flourish,

They flourish only to be destroyed for ever;
    but you, O LORD, are exalted for evermore.

For lo, your enemies, O LORD,
lo, your enemies shall perish,
        and all the workers of iniquity shall be scattered.

But my horn you have exalted like the horns of wild bulls;
    I am anointed with fresh oil.

My eyes also gloat over my enemies,
        and my ears rejoice to hear the doom of the wicked who
            rise up against me.

The righteous shall flourish like a palm tree,
    and shall spread abroad like a cedar of Lebanon.

Those who are planted in the house of the LORD
    shall flourish in the courts of our God;

They shall still bear fruit in old age;
    they shall be green and succulent;

That they may show how upright the LORD is,
    my Rock, in whom there is no fault.

PSALM 93

If you want to sing praises on Friday, you have the praise in Psalm 93. On that day the crucifixion took place and the house of God was built even though the enemies tried to prevent it. For this reason, it is fitting to sing to God these words as a song of victory.

The LORD is King;
he has put on splendid apparel;
    the LORD has put on his apparel
    and girded himself with strength.

He has made the whole world so sure
    that it cannot be moved;

Ever since the world began, your throne has been established;
    you are from everlasting.

The waters have lifted up, O LORD,
the waters have lifted up their voice;
    the waters have lifted up their pounding waves.

Mightier than the sound of many waters,
mightier than the breakers of the sea,
    mightier is the LORD who dwells on high.

Your testimonies are very sure,
    and holiness adorns your house, O LORD,
    for ever and for evermore.

∽ PSALM 94

Do you want to sing on Wednesday? You have Psalm 94. On that day the Lord was betrayed and began to take vengeance against death and to triumph over it courageously. So whenever you read the Gospel and see on Wednesday the Jews conspiring against the Lord, and you see him on that day boldly confronting the devil on your behalf, sing these words.

O Lord God of vengeance,
    O God of vengeance, show yourself.

Rise up, O Judge of the world;
    give the arrogant their just deserts.

How long shall the wicked, O Lord,
    how long shall the wicked triumph?

They bluster in their insolence;
    all evildoers are full of boasting.

They crush your people, O Lord,
    and afflict your chosen nation.

They murder the widow and the stranger
    and put the orphans to death.

Yet they say, "The Lord does not see,
    the God of Jacob takes no notice."

Consider well, you dullards among the people;
    when will you fools understand?

He that planted the ear, does he not hear?
    he that formed the eye, does he not see?

He who admonishes the nations, will he not punish?
    he who teaches all the world, has he no knowledge?

The Lord knows our human thoughts;
    how like a puff of wind they are.

Happy are they whom you instruct, O Lord!
  whom you teach out of your law;

To give them rest in evil days,
  until a pit is dug for the wicked.

For the LORD will not abandon his people,
  nor will he forsake his own.

For judgment will again be just,
  and all the true of heart will follow it.

Who rose up for me against the wicked?
  who took my part against the evildoers?

If the LORD had not come to my help,
  I should soon have dwelt in the land of silence.

As often as I said, "My foot has slipped,"
  your love, O LORD, upheld me.

When many cares fill my mind,
  your consolations cheer my soul.

Can a corrupt tribunal have any part with you,
  one which frames evil into law?

They conspire against the life of the just
  and condemn the innocent to death.

But the LORD has become my stronghold,
  and my God the rock of my trust.

He will turn their wickedness back upon them
and destroy them in their own malice;
  the LORD our God will destroy them.

⌐ PSALM 96

If after being in captivity the house of God was destroyed and then later rebuilt, sing the words in Psalm 96.

Sing to the LORD a new song;
  sing to the LORD, all the whole earth.

Sing to the LORD and bless his Name;
  proclaim the good news of his salvation from day to day.

Declare his glory among the nations
  and his wonders among all peoples.

For great is the LORD and greatly to be praised;
  he is more to be feared than all gods.

As for all the gods of the nations, they are but idols;
  but it is the LORD who made the heavens.

Oh, the majesty and magnificence of his presence!
  Oh, the power and the splendor of his sanctuary!

Ascribe to the LORD, you families of the peoples;
  ascribe to the LORD honor and power.

Ascribe to the LORD the honor due his Name;
  bring offerings and come into his courts.

Worship the LORD in the beauty of holiness;
  let the whole earth tremble before him.

Tell it out among the nations: "The LORD is King!
  he has made the world so firm that it cannot be moved;
  he will judge the peoples with equity."

Let the heavens rejoice, and let the earth be glad;
let the sea thunder and all that is in it;
  let the field be joyful and all that is therein.

Then shall all the trees of the wood shout for joy
before the LORD when he comes,
>   when he comes to judge the earth.

He will judge the world with righteousness
>   and the peoples with his truth.

～ PSALM 97

When the earth receives rest after being at war and remains peaceful,
and the Lord rules, if you want to sing about this, you have Psalm 97.

The LORD is King;
let the earth rejoice;
>   let the multitude of the isles be glad.

Clouds and darkness are round about him,
>   righteousness and justice are the foundations of his throne.

A fire goes before him
>   and burns up his enemies on every side.

His lightnings light up the world;
>   the earth sees it and is afraid.

The mountains melt like wax at the presence of the LORD,
>   at the presence of the Lord of the whole earth.

The heavens declare his righteousness,
>   and all the peoples see his glory.

Confounded be all who worship carved images
and delight in false gods!
>   Bow down before him, all you gods.

Zion hears and is glad, and the cities of Judah rejoice,
>   because of your judgments, O LORD.

For you are the LORD,
most high over all the earth;
    you are exalted far above all gods.

The LORD loves those who hate evil;
    he preserves the lives of his saints
    and delivers them from the hand of the wicked.

Light has sprung up for the righteous,
    and joyful gladness for those who are truehearted.

Rejoice in the LORD, you righteous,
    and give thanks to his holy Name.

⁓ PSALM 108

For expressing lasting faithfulness in a song, sing Psalm 108.

My heart is firmly fixed, O God, my heart is fixed;
    I will sing and make melody.

Wake up, my spirit;
awake, lute and harp;
    I myself will waken the dawn.

I will confess you among the peoples, O LORD;
    I will sing praises to you among the nations.

For your loving-kindness is greater than the heavens,
    and your faithfulness reaches to the clouds.

Exalt yourself above the heavens, O God,
    and your glory over all the earth.

So that those who are dear to you may be delivered,
    save with your right hand and answer me.

God spoke from his holy place and said,
    "I will exult and parcel out Shechem;
    I will divide the valley of Succoth.

Gilead is mine and Manasseh is mine;
    Ephraim is my helmet and Judah my scepter.

Moab is my washbasin,
on Edom I throw down my sandal to claim it,
    and over Philistia will I shout in triumph."

Who will lead me into the strong city?
    who will bring me into Edom?

Have you not cast us off, O God?
    you no longer go out, O God, with our armies.

Grant us your help against the enemy,
    for vain is the help of man.

With God we will do valiant deeds,
    and he shall tread our enemies under foot.

⌢ PSALM 116:9–17*

Do you have faith, as the Lord said, and do you believe the things you
say while praying? Say Psalm 116:9–17.

I believed, even when I said,
"I have been brought very low."
    In my distress I said, "No one can be trusted."

How shall I repay the LORD
    for all the good things he has done for me?

I will lift up the cup of salvation
    and call upon the Name of the LORD.

* Psalm 115 of Athanasius's LXX version corresponds to Psalm 116:9–17 of the BCP.

I will fulfill my vows to the LORD
    in the presence of all his people.

Precious in the sight of the LORD
    is the death of his servants.

O LORD, I am your servant;
    I am your servant and the child of your handmaid;
    you have freed me from my bonds.

I will offer you the sacrifice of thanksgiving
    and call upon the Name of the LORD.

I will fulfill my vows to the LORD
    in the presence of all his people,

In the courts of the LORD's house,
    in the midst of you, O Jerusalem.
    Hallelujah!

⌐ PSALM 143

Do you want to make a request and pray? Sing Psalms 5 and 143.

LORD, hear my prayer,
and in your faithfulness heed my supplications;
    answer me in your righteousness.

Enter not into judgment with your servant,
    for in your sight shall no one living be justified.

For my enemy has sought my life;
he has crushed me to the ground;
    he has made me live in dark places like those who
        are long dead.

My spirit faints within me;
    my heart within me is desolate.

I remember the time past;
I muse upon all your deeds;
    I consider the works of your hands.
I spread out my hands to you;
     my soul gasps to you like a thirsty land.

O Lord, make haste to answer me; my spirit fails me;
    do not hide your face from me
    or I shall be like those who go down to the Pit.

Let me hear of your loving-kindness in the morning,
for I put my trust in you;
    show me the road that I must walk,
    for I lift up my soul to you.

Deliver me from my enemies, O Lord,
    for I flee to you for refuge.

Teach me to do what pleases you, for you are my God;
    let your good Spirit lead me on level ground.

Revive me, O Lord, for your Name's sake;
    for your righteousness' sake, bring me out of trouble.

Of your goodness, destroy my enemies
and bring all my foes to naught,
    for truly I am your servant.

AFTERWORD

The Psalms are the prayer book of the church. Here the temple liturgy is sung. Here God's providential arrangement of the days, nights, and all the seasons is ritualized. Here the movements of the human heart find their deepest expression. In finding their own voices in the Psalms, the first Christians came to hear Christ crying out on every page. That these hymns were written many centuries before the coming of Christ in no way deterred the early church because in them they found mysteries illuminated only by the light of the Incarnation.

As such, patristic commentaries on the Psalms are numerous: Origen, Eusebius of Caesarea, Asterius, Hilary, Didymus, the Cappadocians, Jerome, Diodore of Tarsus, Hesychius of Jerusalem, Theodore of Mopsuestia, John Chrysostom, Cyril of Alexandria, Cassiodorus, and Augustine of Hippo all began commentaries on the Psalms. While some of these have come down to us in toto, most are known only partially through excerpts in the writings of other medieval figures.

These excerpts have enabled scholars to re-create Athanasius's commentaries on the hymns of David; and in his widely influential *Letter to Marcellinus*, we read how Christ is ultimately the meaning found in every psalm. Better than most, St. Athanasius saw how in the Psalms Christians could come to understand both the person and the work of Jesus at every turn, as the book of Psalms

knew Christ himself as the Coming One and indeed it especially speaks concerning him in the forty-fourth psalm. . . . And lest someone suppose that he comes only in semblance, it makes clear that this same one will become man and that this is he through whom all things were made, as it says in Psalm 86. . . . On this account also, since it knows that this was from a virgin, the Psalter was not silent, but immediately gives some clear expression. . . . For indeed, having stated that he is Christ, soon thereafter it made known the human birth from the virgin in saying, *Hear, O daughter* (Psalm 44:10). Take note that Gabriel calls Mary by name, since he is dissimilar to her in terms of origination, but David the Psalmist properly addresses her as *daughter*, because she happened to be from his seed (Athanasius, *Letter to Marcellinus* 6).

In this way the great bishop of Alexandria allows David the king of Israel to introduce him to his own Lord and Savior. In this interaction, then, the early church learns to read not only the Psalms but also the whole Old Testament as the place where Christian salvation is being prepared. Israel flowers into the new daughter Mary and from her comes the One whom every child of Adam and Eve await.

Ben Wayman reinvigorates the ancient voice of Athanasius, a true pastor of souls, by allowing him to speak tenderly to his flock, even today. Thanks to Wayman, Athanasius speaks not as the intrepid theologian facing down emperors and heretics, as history usually too facilely remembers him—*Athanasius contra mundum*—but as one who cares for his flock and seeks ways to allow the Scriptures to come alive for them. Athanasius was a man who knew his people intimately and was a bishop who saw his role as mediating the mysteries of the Bible with the everyday practicalities of the hungry flock before him.

Accordingly, Wayman represents the Psalms in eight main sections. Each section brings to life the Psalms on which Athanasius preached in order to help his people see themselves and the movements of their hearts. Wayman's book draws the reader into the ritualization of the human condition in the Psalms, providing liturgical hymns for practically any experience.

There are psalms for the suffering, for those who, like the anguished Christ, long to hear the Father's voice. There are psalms for those who have been betrayed; for those who—like Jesus—have been rejected by those they once called friends, and await the Father's embrace. There are psalms for the harassed as well as the guilty, for those who seek reconciliation and to know deeply God's forgiveness and acceptance.

The thankful will find psalms to capture and channel the praise of those who see all that God does around and in them. Because Athanasius knew well the very practical ways the Psalms can lead those humble enough to listen, there are psalms for reflection and instruction. Finally, what Wayman names the psalms for daily life round out this work's brilliance, as the reader comes to understand God's invitation to wholeness as each day unfolds.

Scholars of late antiquity and regular readers of the Bible owe Dr. Wayman thanks for his labors throughout this volume. His translations of Athanasius's counsel are alluring and accurate, prayerful and powerful. This guide to the Psalms hence aims to bring its readers into contact not only with Athanasius, the greatest Greek theologian of the church, but also ultimately with the living God, who is the true author of the preceding pages.

Fr. David V. Meconi, sj
Assistant Professor of Patristic Theology
Saint Louis University

NOTES

1 Clebsch 1980, xviii.
2 Balás and Bingham 2006, 299.
3 Lewis 2011, 11.
4 This description is a paraphrase of Clebsch 1980, xiii.
5 Pamela Bright has helped recover the work for modern readers with her recent translation and study. Praising Athanasius's *Letter*, she states, "Such a piece of spiritual hermeneutics . . . is a unique treasure unparalleled in the literature of the patristic era." Bright 1986, 19.
6 See Ferguson 1978, 380–81, who identifies this connection.
7 Basil of Caesarea, "Homilia in psalmum primum," PG 29:212a, trans. Jackson 1994, xlv.
8 Athanasius, *Epistola ad Marcellinum*, PG 27:28c, trans. Bright 1986, 66 (slightly altered).
9 Ferguson 1978, 378.
10 Ferguson 1978, 381. Ferguson notes in addition that "the *Opusculum* was printed in Latin translation in the sixteenth century before the other works of Athanasius were printed."
11 Ferguson maintains, "Athanasius' *Epistola ad Marcellinum* (MG 27.12–45) has received little published study" (1985, 295).
12 Leithart 2011, 15. Gregg similarly contends that Athanasius "became one of the most vivid and forceful personalities in fourth-century ecclesiastical and political affairs" (1980, 1). Timothy Barnes likens Athanasius to a "modern gangster" and credits him with organizing "an ecclesiastical mafia" (1981, 230). See also Barnes 1993, 1–3.
13 Gwynn 2012, 3. cf. Rufinus's *Historia Ecclesiastica* 10.15 and the *History of the Patriarchs of Alexandria*, belonging to the Egyptian Coptic tradition (see Gwynn 2012, 1–5).
14 In his study of "Arianism" and fourth-century Christianity, Rowan Williams states, "The crisis of the fourth century was the most dramatic internal struggle the Christian Church had so far experienced" (2002, 1).
15 Julian, "To the Alexandrians," Letter 47, 435d, and Julian, "To Ecdicius, Prefect of Egypt," Letter 46, 376a, trans. Gregg 1980, xii.
16 Concerning Julian "the Apostate," Gwynn makes the noteworthy observation that "in October 362 he [Athanasius] received the rare accolade of being one of the few bishops to be forced into exile by the last pagan emperor" (2002, 16).

17 Rowan Williams underlines Athanasius's ability to ally the eastern episcopate with the monastic movement, and how his "'monasticizing' of bishops could lead to the politicizing of monasticism" (2002, 90). Similarly, Khaled Anatolios observes that "Athanasius' lifetime also saw the beginning and dramatic rise of the monastic movement in Egypt, and it would be part of the achievement of his episcopate to transform this conglomeration of desert-dwellers who were suspicious of authority and its pomp into a fairly cohesive group who were intensely loyal to him and zealous for doctrinal orthodoxy" (2004, 2–3).

18 Gwynn states that the *"Orationes contra Arianos* form Athanasius' most extensive work of theology and polemic" (2002, 10).

19 William Clebsch considers the *Vita Antonii*, which narrates "the life of the hermit-monk Antony" to be "the most influential writing by Athanasius, despite the cardinal importance of his doctrinal tract *On the Incarnation of the Word of God"* (1980, xiii). Khaled Anatolios states that in the *Life of Antony* (ca. 356), "the great Egyptian monk is presented as a model of Athanasius's own conception of Nicene orthodoxy" (2004, 30).

20 The *Tomus ad Antiochenos* was Athanasius's attempt to resolve the divisions in Antioch, which stemmed from multiple claims to the episcopate by pro-Nicene camps and various others in the city.

21 Rowan Williams has argued convincingly that Athanasius prevailed over Arius largely due to his more pastoral approach as a church theologian in contrast to Arius, who acted as a "school" theologian. See Williams 2002, esp. 82–91. Williams will thus state, "Part of his [Arius's] tragedy is that (even among his allies) the tradition of such school-centered Christianity is a dying one" (2002, 85). Williams describes Athanasius's approach as "Catholic" and Arius's approach as "Academic" (see Williams 2002, 87).

22 Pamela Bright observes that "the young Athanasius, probably not yet thirty years old, was chosen as the occupant of the most influential see among all the Christian churches at that time" (1986, 11).

23 Pamela Bright has noted that from a careful reading of his writings, "the surprising fact begins to emerge that even in the more polemic *Apologies,* Athanasius is revealed as a pastor, much less interested in imperial politics than in the religious and spiritual education of his flock. If correctly noted, this primary concern reveals in all the Athanasian treatises and letters a vivid interest in the Bible and its use in a pastoral pedagogy" (1986, 12).

24 Paul Kolbet states, "The interpreter of Athanasius's letter should, therefore, be aware that Athanasius's Nicene christology informs and shapes his advice to Marcellinus" (2006, 93).

25 Marcellinus's identity is unknown, and the name was common during Athanasius's time. However, Robert Gregg draws attention to "Athanasius' *Apologia c. Arianos* 73, which lists a Marcellinus among the deacons of Alexandria" (1980, 21; see also 134). I have accordingly decided to presume that at the least, Marcellinus was a Christian under Athanasius's pastoral care.

26 Athanasius, *Epistola ad Marcellinum*, PG 27:20d, trans. Sr. Penelope 1953, 103 (emphasis original).

27 Athanasius, *Epistola ad Marcellinum*, PG 27:21a, trans. Gregg 1980, 108.

28 Athanasius, *Epistola ad Marcellinum*, PG 27:25c, trans. Ferguson 1978, 391.

29 Robert Gregg states, "The document testifies on every page to Athanasius's conviction, which he sought to foster in those to whom he was pastor, of the central and sustaining force of the recitation of the Psalms in the experience of Christian people" (1980, 25).

30 Weinandy 2010, 275. Everett Ferguson similarly suggests a date in the 360s. See Ferguson 1985, 295–96.

31 Athanasius spent his third and fourth exiles with the desert monks. Concerning Athanasius's third exile, for example, Gwynn notes, "Athanasius spent much of the period 356–62 in the company of the desert ascetics" (2012, 15). See also Kolbet 2006, 89–90, who suggests that desert monastic traditions likely informed Athanasius's counsel to Marcellinus.

32 Not to mention *Athanasius's* interpretation of Scripture. Pamela Bright notes that despite being "an inspired interpreter of Scripture, Athanasius has not transmitted in his literary legacy a single commentary on a book of the Old or New Testament" (1986, 12). Thus it is significant that "the *Letter to Marcellinus* is the only surviving complete Athanasian work dealing exclusively with Scripture and its interpretation" (Gregg 1980, 19).

33 Athanasius, *Epistola ad Marcellinum*, PG 27:20c, trans. Bright 1986, 61 (slightly altered).

34 Commenting on Athanasius's letter, Khaled Anatolios states, "This practice of applying the Scriptures to the various circumstances of one's life seems to have been a mainstay of Athanasius's spirituality. Nothing is more characteristic of his approach than the tendency to render every situation and every question into scriptural categories, and to assimilate contemporary persons with scriptural personages" (2004, 37).

35 Athanasius, *Epistola ad Marcellinum*, PG 27:24b, trans. Ferguson 1978, 390.

36 Athanasius, *Epistola ad Marcellinum*, PG 27:24a-b, trans. Bright 1986, 63.

37 Hays 2007, 12 (emphasis original). In this respect, Athanasius's approach is akin to what Richard Hays calls "theological exegesis," which entails reading Scripture "with an awareness that we are addressed and claimed by the

word of God that is spoken in the text, and we understand ourselves to be answerable to that word" (2007, 12). Athanasius would likely agree with Hays that reading the Psalms in this way is "closely interwoven with the practice of *worship*" (2007, 12 [emphasis original]).

38 Athanasius, *Epistola ad Marcellinum*, PG 27:21b, trans. Bright 1986, 62.

39 See my discussion of Athanasius's commitment to the actual words (λέξεις and λόγους) of the Psalms in *Diodore the Theologian* (2014, 126-131).

40 Athanasius, *Epistola ad Marcellinum*, PG 27:25b, trans. Ferguson 1978, 391.

41 Athanasius, *Epistola ad Marcellinum*, PG 27:28d, trans. Sr. Penelope 1953, 107.

42 Athanasius, *Epistola ad Marcellinum*, PG 27:41d–44a, trans. Ferguson 1978, 400–401.

43 Athanasius, *Epistola ad Marcellinum*, PG 27:44a, trans. Sr. Penelope 1953, 116–17.

44 To be sure, Athanasius sharply opposed elitism in the church. Pamela Bright explains, "Athanasian spirituality claims that the divine revelation, communicated by Scripture, is given to all the faithful in common and at once, and is mediated for them by the church itself by its rites, its sacraments, and its true openness to the gospel message. . . . Athanasius never made a special case for the hierarchical ministry of the church. He saw the church as instrumental for everyone's access to the complete truth of Scripture" (1986, 13).

45 Athanasius, *Epistola ad Marcellinum*, PG 27:44a–b, trans. Bright 1986, 75.

46 For example, it is possible that in addition to the patriarchs, prophets, and apostles, Athanasius has in mind Antony when he states that by speaking the words of the Psalter one "will overturn the Devil and drive away his demons." Athanasius, *Epistola ad Marcellinum*, PG 27:44b, trans. Ferguson 1978, 401. See the *Life of Antony*, for example, where Antony states, "As I prayed and lay chanting psalms to myself, they [the demons] immediately began to wail and cry out, as though they were severely weakened, and I glorified the Lord, who came and made an example of their audacity and madness" (Athanasius, *Vita Antonii*, PG 26:901a, trans. Gregg 1980, 61).

47 Athanasius, *Epistola ad Marcellinum*, PG 27:45a, trans. Bright 1986, 76 (emphasis mine).

48 Athanasius, *Epistola ad Marcellinum*, PG 27:44d, trans. Ferguson 1978, 402.

49 Athanasius, *Epistola ad Marcellinum*, PG 27:45a (my translation).

50 Athanasius, *Epistola ad Marcellinum*, PG 27:45c, trans. Ferguson 1978, 403.

51 Although Athanasius references every psalm in his letter, he does not provide specific direction for each psalm individually. Several psalms he groups in long lists that fall under broad categories (such as the fifteen Psalms of

Ascent: Pss. 120–34) are not covered by Athanasius. Thus, Athanasius's *Guide* does not include Psalms 49, 60, 61, 68, 80, 120–26, 129–34.

52 See Everett Ferguson 1985, 296, who discusses the letter according to the "devotional, liturgical, Christological, doctrinal, and catechetical uses of the Psalms." Though he notes, "The devotional use of the Psalms seems to be what predominates in this letter" (1985, 300).

53 Everett Ferguson rightly observes, "The use of the Psalms in the daily office is reflected at several points, although no distinction is made in the comments between a private and a church use" (1985, 300). The Psalms reflecting the daily office can be found in chapter 8 of Athanasius's *Guide*, titled "Psalms for Daily Life."

54 τούτῳ καθηγεμόνι. Athanasius, *Epistola ad Marcellinum*, PG 27:40b.

55 Athanasius, *Epistola ad Marcellinum*, PG 27:41c–d, trans. Bright 1986, 75.

56 Athanasius, *Epistola ad Marcellinum*, PG 27:24d, trans. Bright 1986, 64 (emphasis mine).

57 Kolbet similarly maintains that Athanasius's letter commends "a daily regime of Psalms to be taken on voluntarily as spiritual exercises to conform the self to a certain ideal. . . . The Psalms are a tool that one uses "to form" or "model oneself" (τυπῶ ἑαυτὸν) (2006, 89).

58 Indeed, for Athanasius "the saying of the Psalms is something like learning a second language. As one becomes a fluent speaker of the language of the Psalms, one is able to linguistically transcribe the *world* into Biblical *words* . . . the very language of the Psalms . . . [is] a formative influence in the Christian life" (Kolbet 2006, 97–98).

SELECTED BIBLIOGRAPHY

Ancient writings

Athanasius of Alexandria. *Epistula ad Marcellinum*. PG 27:12–45.

―――. *Vita Antonii*. PG 26:835–976.

Basil of Caesarea. "Homilia in psalmum primum." In *Homiliae super psalmos*. PG 29:209a–213c.

Julian. "To Ecdicius, Prefect of Egypt." Letter 46. In *Julian III*, 376a. Translated by W. C. Wright. Edited by J. Henderson. Loeb Classical Library 157. Cambridge, MA: Harvard University Press, 1923.

―――. "To the Alexandrians." Letter 47. In *Julian III*, 435d. Translated by W. C. Wright. Edited by J. Henderson. Loeb Classical Library 157. Cambridge, MA: Harvard University Press, 1923.

Modern translations and studies

Anatolios, Khaled. 2004. *Athanasius*. The Early Church Fathers. London: Routledge.

Balás, David L., and D. Jeffrey Bingham. 2006. "Psalms." In *Handbook of Patristic Exegesis: The Bible in Ancient Christianity*. Edited by Charles Kannengiesser, 297–301. Leiden: Brill.

Barnes, Timothy D. 1981. *Constantine and Eusebius*. Cambridge, MA: Harvard University Press.

―――. 1993. *Athanasius and Constantius: Theology and Politics in the Constantinian Empire*. Cambridge, MA: Harvard University Press.

Bright, Pamela, trans. 1986. "Athanasius of Alexandria: On the Interpretation of the Psalms." In *Early Christian Spirituality*. Edited by Charles Kannengiesser, 56–77. Philadelphia: Fortress.

Clebsch, William A. 1980. Preface to *Athanasius: The Life of Antony and the Letter to Marcellinus*. Translated by R. C. Gregg. New York: Paulist Press.

Ferguson, Everett, trans. 1978. "Athanasius, *Epistola ad Marcellinum in interpretationem psalmorum*." *Ekklesiastikos Pharos*, 378–403.

———. 1985. "Athanasius' '*Epistola ad Marcellinum in interpretationem Psalmorum*.'" *Studia Patristica* 16, no. 2:295–308.

Gregg, Robert C., trans. 1980. *Athanasius: The Life of Antony and the Letter to Marcellinus*. New York: Paulist Press.

Gwynn, David M. 2012. *Athanasius of Alexandria: Bishop, Theologian, Ascetic, Father*. Oxford: Oxford University Press.

Hays, Richard B. 2007. "Reading the Bible with Eyes of Faith: The Practice of Theological Exegesis." In *Journal of Theological Interpretation* 1, no. 1:5–21.

Jackson, Blomfield, trans. 1994. *Basil: Letters and Select Works*. Edited by P. Schaff and H. Wace. Nicene and Post-Nicene Fathers, series 2, vol. 8. Peabody, MA: Hendrickson.

Kolbet, Paul R. 2006. "Athanasius, the Psalms, and the Reformation of the Self." *Harvard Theological Review* 99, no. 1:85–101.

Leithart, Peter J. 2011. *Athanasius*. Foundations of Theological Exegesis and Christian Spirituality. Grand Rapids: Baker Academic.

Lewis, C. S. 2011. Preface to *St. Athanasius the Great of Alexandria: On the Incarnation*, Popular Patristic Series 44a. Translated with an introduction by John Behr. Yonkers, NY: St. Vladimir's Seminary Press.

Pietersma, Albert, trans. 2007. "Psalm 151." In *A New English Translation of the Septuagint*. Edited by Albert Pietersma and Benjamin G. Wright, 619–20. Oxford: Oxford University Press.

Sr. Penelope, trans. 1953. "The Letter of St. Athanasius to Marcellinus *On the Interpretation of the Psalms*." In *St. Athanasius: On the Incarnation, The Treatise De incarnatione verbi Dei*. Crestwood, NY: St. Vladimir's Seminary Press.

Wayman, Benjamin D. 2014. *Diodore the Theologian: Πρόνοια in his Commentary on Psalms 1–50*. Studia Traditionis Theologiae 15. Turnhout: Brepols.

Weinandy, Thomas G. 2010. "Athanasius' Letter to Marcellinus: A Soteriological Praying of the Psalms." *Studia Patristica* 46:275–79.

Williams, Rowan. 2002 *Arius: Heresy and Tradition*. 2nd ed. Grand Rapids: Eerdmans.

ABOUT PARACLETE PRESS

Who We Are

Paraclete Press is a publisher of books, recordings, and DVDs on Christian spirituality. Our publishing represents a full expression of Christian belief and practice—from Catholic to Evangelical, from Protestant to Orthodox.

We are the publishing arm of the Community of Jesus, an ecumenical monastic community in the Benedictine tradition. As such, we are uniquely positioned in the marketplace without connection to a large corporation and with informal relationships to many branches and denominations of faith.

What We Are Doing

Paraclete Press Books

Paraclete publishes books that show the richness and depth of what it means to be Christian. Although Benedictine spirituality is at the heart of all that we do, we publish books that reflect the Christian experience across many cultures, time periods, and houses of worship. We publish books that nourish the vibrant life of the church and its people—books about spiritual practice, formation, history, ideas, and customs.

We have several different series, including the best-selling Paraclete Essentials and Paraclete Giants series of classic texts in contemporary English; Voices from the Monastery—men and women monastics writing about living a spiritual life today; award-winning poetry; best-selling gift books for children on the occasions of baptism and first communion; and the Active Prayer Series that brings creativity and liveliness to any life of prayer.

Mount Tabor Books

Paraclete's Mount Tabor Books series focuses on liturgical worship, art and art history, ecumenism, and the first millennium church.

Paraclete Recordings

From Gregorian chant to contemporary American choral works, our music recordings celebrate sacred choral music through the centuries. Paraclete Recordings is the record label of the internationally acclaimed choir Gloriæ Dei Cantores, praised for their "rapt and fathomless spiritual intensity" by *American Record Guide,* and the Gloriæ Dei Cantores Schola, which specializes in the study and performance of Gregorian chant. Paraclete Press is also the exclusive North American distributor of the recordings of the Monastic Choir of St. Peter's Abbey in Solesmes, France, long considered to be a leading authority on Gregorian chant.

Paraclete Video Productions

Our DVDs offer spiritual help, healing, and biblical guidance for life issues: grief and loss, marriage, forgiveness, anger management, facing death, and spiritual formation.

Learn more about us at our website
www.paracletepress.com or
phone us toll-free at 1.800.451.5006

SCAN
TO
READ
MORE

You may also enjoy these products from
Paraclete Press . . .

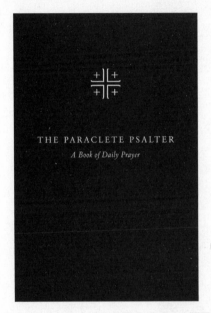

THE PARACLETE PSALTER
A Book of Daily Prayer

ISBN: 978-1-55725-663-8 | $29.99, Bonded Leather

For two thousand years the Psalms have been used as a method of daily prayer in the Liturgy of the Hours. This book is intended for use as a prayer book or a breviary for individuals not able to participate in the public prayers of churches or monastic communities. All 150 psalms are included in a four-week prayer cycle.

THOU ART MY REFUGE
Psalms of Salvation and Mercy

GDCD 038
ISBN: 978-1-55725-451-1 | $16.95

HE HAS HEARD MY VOICE
Psalms of Faithfulness and Hope

GDCD 043
ISBN: 978-1-55725-547-1 | $18.95

HIS LOVE ENDURES FOREVER
Psalms of Thankfulness and Praise

GDCD 045
ISBN: 978-1-55725-593-8 | $18.95

Prefect for contemplative listening at any place or time, this three-volume series plumbs the spiritual depth and beautiful poetry of the psalms as sung in the tradition of Anglican Psalmody. Gloriæ Dei Cantores, who inherited its edition of Psalmody from Dr. George Guest of Cambridge University, England, provides a wealth of experience in the communication of the rich texts of these psalms using the Coverdale translation. The program notes include devotional material on each psalm, making these recordings a valuable tool for private devotion.

Available from most booksellers or through Paraclete Press:
www.paracletepress.com   1-800-451-5006
Try your local bookstore first.